AFFILIATE MARKETING FOR BEGINNERS 2021

The Ultimate Guide To Succeed in
Advertising, Master this Social Media,
Grow your Brand, Get Customers,
your Sales and Profits as Passive

Gary Godin and Allan Kennedy

TABLE OF CONTENTS

INTRODUCTION

The standard entrepreneur told me it's not possible to win using search engine optimization to rank my website. So did everybody else.

In fact, everyone I have spoken to since I started creating my blogs for affiliate marketing told me I wouldn't achieve any success.

They were wrong.

But it wasn't them or their words that helped me. It was me, my pain, my studies and my hunger, that boosted my work...and now here we are, me teaching you how to win with an affiliate marketing business.

After all, you don't know where to start, or how to structure your business, or if your business idea is good enough, or if you have enough to say, or if anyone will care once you launch it. And then there's the worst fear of all, the one you don't want to talk about but always lingers:

What if you start a bad affiliate marketing business?

You might have even started thinking about the website at some point, but you stopped. You probably had some good momentum at first and found it really rewarding to get your ideas out of your head. You thought about how people would see your business, maybe pictured the eventual praise in your future. But you hit an obstacle, and it stalled you. It brought up all your self-doubt and anxiety, and without a plan to get past that obstacle (or obstacles), you lost your momentum, and then you stopped.

It's probably frustrating that you aren't running your business. You see other people—some of whom don't even know as much as you about your subject—who did launch their businesses, who have credibility and authority in their field, who are getting increased visibility, and who have more clients and more opportunities, all from their affiliate marketing structure. Most of all, you see the impact their businesses have on people.

You know you could have that same impact—if you could just get your business done. Your book might not save the world, but it could change some people's lives for the better…if only you could get it to them.

Does this sound familiar? Does it describe you? If so, then this is the perfect book for you.

It was written specifically for people just like you, as you embark on your journey to running and boosting with affiliate marketing strategies in your own business. If you follow the steps, it will get you there.

What is Affiliate Marketing?

I'm going to give you a quick definition of affiliate marketing, in the following pages and chapters we will better understand what affiliate marketing is and how it works.

Affiliate marketing is a marketing arrangement by which an on-line retailer pays commission to an external website for traffic or sales generated from its referrals.

What This Book Will Teach You

In this book, I will teach you everything you need to know to make sure you run and scale a great website—one that impacts readers lives or your business. Here's just a sample of how-to topics you'll find in these pages:

- How affiliate marketing really works
- What's the right mindset to win having an affiliate marketing business
- How this book can help your business
- How to succeed in affiliate marketing campaigns
- How to set up a powerful website for affiliate conversions
- How to win by building great channels for your business
- How to combine social media with affiliate marketing
- How to become an online marketing expert
- How to fix common problems with affiliate marketing
- How to integrate affiliate marketing for your Instagram page

- How to integrate affiliate marketing for your blog
- How to integrate affiliate marketing for your YouTube channel
- How to define and use the 16affiliate marketing networks

How to Approach This Book

Everything you'll read in this book has been tested over years.

This method has been proven to work at the highest levels of online marketing and brand positioning, and with regular people who are not professional marketers. The point is, you're in good hands.

This doesn't mean that only by reading this book you will get success on your website by doing nothing. This is only the first step in your way to success with your affiliate marketing business.

It doesn't take an hour or a day, or a week to see great results thanks to affiliate marketing, it's a long term game. It takes action and action again, everyday. We will better cover this in chapter 2 about the right mindset you need to win with an affiliate marketing business.

Every effort has been made to accurately represent this book and its potential. In terms of earnings, there is no guarantee that you will earn any money using the techniques and ideas in this book. Information presented on this book is not to be interpreted as a promise or guarantee of earnings. Earning potential is entirely dependent on the person using our strategies, ideas and techniques.

Your level of success in getting the results claimed inside this book depends only on the time you devote to the strategy, ideas and techniques mentioned, your knowledge, finances, and various skills. Since these factors differ from individual to individual, we cannot guarantee your success or income level.

Many factors are going to be important in determining your actual results and no guarantees are made that you will simply achieve results almost like ours or anyone else.

Now, let's get started.

CHAPTER ONE

WHAT AFFILIATE MARKETING IS AND HOW IT WORKS

Waking up at a time someone else decides? Going to the office through traffic jams with streets clogged with other sleepy commuters? Spending a boring 8 hours in the office until sweet release at 5pm?

Sound terrible?

What if, instead of dealing with the monotony and stupor of the rat race to earn a few bucks, you could make money at any time, from anywhere — even while you sleep?

That's the concept behind affiliate marketing.

Affiliate marketing is a great way to drive sales and create significant online revenue. Extremely beneficial to both affiliate marketers and brands, this strategy is different from traditional marketing tactics and has paid off. In fact:

82% of brands and 85% of publishers leverage the power of affiliate marketing, a statistic that will continue to increase as affiliate marketing spending increases every year in the United States.

There is a 10.1% increase in affiliate marketing spending in the United States each year, meaning that by 2021, that number will reach $6.9 billion.

In 2018, content marketing costs were gauged to be 63% of traditional marketing schemes while simultaneously generating three times the leads of traditional methods. In fact, 17% of all orders made online can be attributed to affiliate marketing campaigns.

In April 2017, Amazon's affiliate structure changed, offering rates of 1-12% of product revenue for creators, providing the opportunity for affiliates to dramatically increase their passive income based on the vertical they're selling on.

The affiliate marketing of Jason Stone, otherwise known as Millionaire Mentor, was responsible for as much as $7 million in retailer sales just in the months of June and July in 2017.

What is Affiliate Marketing?

Affiliate marketing is the process by which an affiliate earns a commission for marketing the products of another company. The affiliate simply looks for a product he or she likes and would suggest to a friend, promotes that product, and earns a commission from every sale he/she makes. Sales are tracked from one website to another through affiliate links.

How does affiliate marketing work?

Because affiliate marketing divides the responsibilities of product marketing and product development between the parties, the skills of a wide variety of people can be used for a more effective marketing strategy while contributors receive a share of the profits. For this to work, there must be three different parties:

Vendors and product developer.

The partner or advertiser.

The consumer.

Let's take a look at the complex relationship of these three parties to ensure affiliate marketing is a success.

1. Seller and product developer.

The seller, be it a sole proprietorship or a large corporation, is a seller, distributor, product developer, or retailer with a product that is being marketed. The product can be a physical object such as household items or a service such as makeup tutorials.

The seller, also referred to as the brand, does not have to be actively involved in marketing, but can also be the advertiser and benefit from the revenue sharing that comes with affiliate marketing.

For example, the seller could be an E-commerce retailer who started a drop shipping business and wants to reach new audiences by paying affiliate websites to promote their products. Or the seller could be a SaaS company that uses partners to help sell their marketing software.

2. The partner or publisher.

The partner, also known as a publisher, can be an individual or a company that markets the seller's product in an attractive way to potential consumers. In other words, the affiliate promotes the product in order to convince consumers that it is valuable or useful to them and to convince them to buy the product. When the consumer buys the product, the partner receives part of the income.

Affiliates often have a very specific audience to market for and generally cater to that audience's interests. This creates a defined niche or personal brand that will help the affiliate attract consumers who are most likely to respond to the advertisement.

3. The consumer.

Whether the consumer knows it or not, they (and their purchases) are the driving forces behind affiliate marketing. Partners share these products with them on social media, blogs, and websites.

When consumers buy the product, the seller and partner share the profit. Sometimes the affiliate chooses to be open to the consumer by announcing that they will receive a commission on the sales they have made. In other cases, the consumer may not even be aware of the affiliate marketing infrastructure behind their purchase.

Regardless, they rarely pay more for the product purchased through affiliate marketing. The affiliated company's share of the profit is included in the sales price. The consumer completes the purchase process and receives the product as usual, without being affected by the affiliate marketing system in which he is involved.

How Do Affiliate Marketers Get Paid?

Affiliate marketing is a fast, inexpensive way to make money without actually selling a product. It is undeniable for those looking to increase their income online. But how does an affiliate get paid after the seller is connected to the consumer?

The answer can get complicated.

The consumer does not always have to buy the product for the partner to suffer a setback. Depending on the program, the partner's contribution to the seller's sales is measured differently.

The partner can be paid in different ways:

1. Pay per sale.

This is the standard affiliate marketing structure. In this program, the merchant pays the partner a percentage of the sales price of the product after the consumer purchases the product based on the partner's marketing strategies. In other words, the partner must actually let the investor invest in the product before getting compensated.

2. Pay per lead.

A more complex system, pay per lead affiliate programs, will compensate the affiliate based on the conversion of leads. The partner must convince the consumer to visit the retailer's website and take the desired action - whether they fill out a contact form, sign up for a trial version of a product, subscribe to a newsletter, or download software or files.

3. Pay per click.

This program focuses on motivating the partner to refer consumers from their marketing platform to the retailer's website. This means that the partner must engage the consumer as they move from the partner's website to the retailer's website. The partner is paid based on the increase in web traffic.

Why Be an Affiliate Marketer?

What Are the Reasons to Become an Affiliate Marketer?

<u>**1. Passive income.**</u>

While any "normal" job requires you to work to make money, affiliate marketing gives you the opportunity to make money while you sleep. If you invest a certain amount of time in a campaign initially, you will see a continuous return at that point as consumers purchase the product in the days and weeks that follow. You get paid for your work long after you finish it. Even when you're away from your computer, your marketing skills will provide you with a steady stream of income.

2. No customer support.

Individual sellers and companies that offer products or services trade with their consumers and ensure that they are satisfied with what they have bought.

Thanks to the affiliate marketing structure, you never have to worry about customer support or customer satisfaction. The entire job of the affiliate marketer is to connect the seller with the consumer. The seller will handle all consumer complaints after receiving your commission on the sale.

3. Work from home.

If you hate going to the office, affiliate marketing is the perfect solution. You can run campaigns and generate income from the products that sellers make at work from the comfort of their homes. This is a job that you can do without ever taking off your pyjamas.

4. Inexpensive.

Most businesses require start-up costs and cash flow to finance the products they sell. Affiliate marketing, however, can be done at a low cost so you can get started quickly and easily. You don't have to worry about the affiliate program or manufacture any product. It is relatively easy to get started with this work.

5. Convenient and flexible.

Since you are essentially freelance, setting your own goals, shifting your path, choosing the products that interest you, and even determining your own hours gives you the ultimate independence. This convenience means you can diversify your portfolio if you prefer simple and straightforward campaigns. You are also free from company restrictions and regulations, as well as underperforming teams.

6. Performance-Based Rewards.

For other jobs, you can work 80 hours a week and still earn the same salary. Affiliate marketing is based entirely on your performance. You get what you put in. By improving your assessment skills and writing engaging campaigns, you can instantly improve your earnings. You are finally getting paid for your excellent work!

7. Don't underestimate the power of search engine optimization.

There is a ton of organic traffic you can get from search engines if you do SEO right. Gone are the days when search engine optimization was all about scamming Google. Today it's all about making your website better for visitors. People naturally look for information online. That's why you need to learn the basics of on-page search engine optimization, keyword research, and link building to be the source of information they find first. Who wouldn't want to be # 1 for terms like "Best Product" or "Product Rating" on Google?

Common Types of Affiliate Marketing Channels

Most affiliates make sure that their audience is receptive to buying the products they are promoting. But not all member companies advertise the products in the same way. In fact, there are several marketing channels that they can use.

1. Influencer

An influencer is a person who can influence the purchasing decision of a large part of the population. This person is in a great position to take advantage of affiliate marketing. They already have an impressive following, making it easy for them to lead consumers about the seller's products through social media posts, blogs, and other interactions with their followers. The influencers then receive a portion of the profit they made.

2. Blogger

With the ability to rank organically in search engine queries, bloggers can increase a seller's conversions. The blogger tries the product of the service and then writes a detailed review that better advertises the brand and drives traffic back to the seller's website.

The blogger is rewarded for their impact on the value of the product on the business, thereby improving the salesperson's sales. For example, my article on the best email marketing software everywhere has product reviews and affiliate links.

3. Paid search-based micro sites

The development and monetization of micro sites can also generate significant revenues. These websites are advertised on a partner page or in the sponsored lists of a search engine. They are different from the location of the main organization. By offering more targeted, relevant content to a specific audience, micro sites achieve more conversions thanks to their simple and clear call to action.

4. Email lists

Despite its older origins, email marketing is still a viable source of income for affiliate marketing. Some partners have email lists that they can use to promote the seller's products. Others can use email newsletters that contain hyperlinks to products and get a commission back after the consumer purchases the product.

Another method is for the partner to build up an email list over time. They use their various campaigns to collect emails and then send emails about the products they promote.

5. Major media websites

These websites are designed to generate a large amount of traffic at all times. You focus on building an audience of millions. These websites promote products to their general audience through banners and contextual affiliate links. This method provides superior engagement and improves conversion rates, resulting in great earnings for both the seller and the partner.

Tips to Help You Become a Successful Affiliate Marketer

1. Develop rapport

When starting your career as an affiliate marketing professional, you want to target audiences with very specific interests. That way, you can tailor your affiliate campaigns to that niche, increasing the chances of conversion. Establishing yourself as an expert in a particular field, rather than promoting a wide variety of products, can help you market it to the people who are most likely to buy the product.

2. Make it personal

There is no shortage of products to advertise. You have the option to choose products that you personally believe in. So make sure your campaigns focus on really valuable products that consumers will like. You will achieve an impressive conversion rate while ensuring the reliability of your personal brand.

You also want to be really good at email reach to collaborate with other bloggers and influencers. Use a tool like ContactOut or Voila Norbert to collect people's contact information and send personalized emails to collect guest blogging and partner opportunities.

3. Start by evaluating products and services

Focus on reviewing products and services that fall into your niche. Then, take advantage of the connection you have established with your audience and your perspective as an expert, and tell your readers why they would benefit from purchasing the product or service you are promoting. Almost anything sold online can be rated if there is an affiliate program in place. You can review physical products, digital software, or even services booked online such as carpooling or travel location booking. It is particularly effective to compare this product with other products in the same category. Most importantly, you generate detailed, clear content to improve conversions.

4. Use different sources

Instead of just focusing on one email campaign, you can also spend time making money on a blog, reaching your audience on social media, and even watching cross-channel promotions.

Test different marketing strategies to see which audience you are best responding to. Use this technique often.

For more information, read this article on How to Start a Successful Blog This Year.

5. Choose campaigns carefully

No matter how good your marketing skills are, you will make less money with a bad product than with a good product. Take the time to research the demand for a product before promoting it. Make sure to research the seller carefully before cooperating. Your time is worth a lot, and you want to make sure you spend it on a product that is profitable and you can believe in.

6. Stay on top of trends

There is serious competition in affiliate marketing. You want to make sure you are always up to date with new trends to stay competitive. Plus, you can probably take advantage of at least some of the new marketing techniques that are constantly being developed. Make sure you are up to date with all of these new strategies to make sure your conversion rates, and therefore sales, are as high as possible.

What are The Main Affiliate Marketing Trends of 2021?

1. Improved partner reporting and allocation

Many affiliate programs run with last-click mapping, where the affiliate who receives the last click before the sale gets 100% credit for the conversion. It changes. With affiliate platforms offering new attribution models and reporting capabilities, you can get a complete, cross-channel view of how individual marketing tactics work together.

For example, you can see that a paid social campaign generated the first click, Affiliate X click 2, and Affiliate Y the last click.

With this complete picture, you can structure your affiliate commissions so that Affiliate X gets a percentage of the credit for the sale, even if they didn't get the last click.

2. Influencer niches are becoming more and more targeted

In the past, key subsidiaries were the mainstay as bulk coupons and media sites brought traffic to hundreds or thousands of advertisers. This is not so much the case anymore. By using long-tail keywords and finding highly specific products and services, influencers can leverage their hyper-targeted niche for affiliate marketing success. Influencers may not be sending advertisers large amounts of traffic, but the audience they're sending is credible, targeted, and has higher conversion rates.

3. GDPR is changing the way in which personal data is collected

The General Data Protection Regulation (GDPR), which came into force on May 25, 2018, is a set of rules that govern the use of personal data across the EU. This forces some partners to receive user data through a declaration of consent (updated privacy policy and cookie statements) even if they are not located in the European Union. These new regulations should also remind you to follow FTC guidelines and clearly state that you will receive affiliate commissions based on your referrals.

4. Affiliate marketers are getting smarter

Merchants who receive a large percentage of their sales through the affiliate channel can become dependent on their affiliate partners.

This can lead affiliate marketers to use their important status to get higher commissions and better deals with their advertisers. Whether it's CPA, CPL, or CPC commission structures, there are many high-paying affiliate programs and affiliate marketers are taking the lead.

What Affiliate Marketing Strategies Should You Use in 2021?

1. Only recommend products that you know well

Building trust with your target audience is paramount in affiliate marketing. The quickest way to lose trust is to recommend products that you haven't used before or that don't suit your audience. Also, make sure you never tell anyone to buy a product directly. You only recommend the product. The more helpful you are and the more you make quality recommendations, the more likely your web visitors will return for your expertise.

2. Promote products from many different retailers

Don't put all your eggs in one basket. If you're only promoting a merchant's products, you're stuck with their commissions, landing pages, and ultimately conversion rates. It's important to partner with many different retailers in your niche to promote a wide variety of products.

This affiliate marketing strategy will diversify the number of your commissions and generate a steady flow of sales as you build an affiliate website. Some examples of affiliate sellers include brands like BigCommerce, Bluehost, and SimplyBook.me.

3. Continuously test and optimize your conversion rates

Let's say you have a promotion page promoting a product through affiliate links. If you are currently receiving 5,000 visits / month with a conversion rate of 2%, you have 100 referrals. To get 200 referrals, you can focus on getting 5,000 more visitors or increase the conversion rate to 4%.

Instead of spending months building domain authority blogging and guest posting to get more organic traffic, just increase your conversion rate by 2%. This may include optimizing the landing page, testing your call to action, and a strategy to optimize the conversion rate. By testing and optimizing your website, you will get much better results with a lot less effort.

4. Focus on your partner traffic sources

Knowing where your traffic is coming from and what your target demographic is, is important. You can customize your messages to give you the best product recommendations for partners. You should focus not only on the industry you are in, but also the traffic sources and the audience visiting your website. Traffic sources can be organic, social media, referral, advertisement, email, or direct traffic.

You can view data from traffic sources in Google Analytics to see, for example, the time on the page, bounce rate, geolocation, age, gender, time of day, devices (mobile or desktop), etc. to focus on the most converting Focus traffic. This analytic data is critical to making informed decisions, increasing your conversion rates, and generating more affiliate sales.

Management Summary

Affiliate marketing is an ideal solution for those who want to take control of their own income by focusing on performance-based income options. By partnering with a seller, a motivated affiliate marketer can generate residual income from the comfort of their own home without having to worry about producing their own product or service.

While the success of the job depends on the affiliate's marketing skills, it can prove to be an effective way to meet your income goals as a primary career or a profitable secondary job.

An elegantly simple process, affiliate marketing through reviews, blogs, social media, webinar software and other platforms, is a new frontier in marketing waiting to be exploited. Follow the tips in this article and you'll be able to engage your audience, convert passive readers into active consumers, and improve your paycheck with one click at a time.

FREQUENTLY ASKED QUESTIONS

I know it's easy to get information overload if you are new to this field. Don't worry, it is natural and part of the process.

You probably have a lot of questions about affiliate marketing. It will be easier for all of us if I answer the most common questions I see.

1. Is it too late for me to start making money from affiliate marketing?

I asked myself the same question in 2008. I thought I had missed the opportunity because ringtones were gradually being regulated, Google stopped Adsense arbitrage and Yahoo Publisher Network lost money. And yet 2009 was the year I ran my first million dollar profit campaigns.

Google started 8 years after Yahoo. Apple made the iPhone ten years after its popularity. Don't worry about being the first ... focus on being the best. If you don't believe you can be successful, then you won't be successful.

"The best time to plant a tree is 20 years ago, the second best time is now" - proverb

In 5 years' time there will be another generation of affiliate marketers who think ... "Man, I wish I had started in 2017."

2. I am not a technical person. I don't know how to code. Can I still be successful in affiliate marketing?

It's 2020. I still don't know how to set up websites or programs. You don't have to be a technical person to be successful. "It's not about what you know, it's about how resourceful you are." You can hire people from Fiverr or Upwork if you need anything.

While being technical helps with the learning curve, it isn't the most important thing. I've seen a lot of programmers and designers in this field who couldn't get affiliate marketing to work. Website programming and design are not the most important skills in affiliate marketing.

The ability to plan, analyze, optimize data, and understand the big picture makes a bigger difference. And the most important skill is marketing.

Guess what ... you can learn all of this easily!

But I think it is worth learning some basic programming skills like PHP and CSS. Sometimes there is a bug on your landing pages and you don't want to wait 8 hours for your freelance programmer to wake up.

3. How much do you need to get started?

When I started out, I was making $ 35,000 a year for one job. After paying my rent, bills, and loans, I had little money left to invest in affiliate marketing. I didn't allow myself to be stopped.

I sold my Xbox and other things I didn't need. I started writing articles for people online for $ 15 per article. I stayed home on the weekends to work instead of going to the clubs. I hurried and was able to save about $ 500 a month. I didn't let any excuse hold me back.

I recommend people have a budget of at least $ 500 per month to invest in this one. There are some resources to invest in such as: B. a tracker and a server. Everything else should be paid for traffic.

Remember, the more money you can invest, the better. Why? Think of it like buying data. When you don't have enough money, you need to worry. Stop complaining. Find a second job. You need money to invest in traffic, servers, tools, and so on. All companies need start-up capital - nothing escapes it.

Do you know what blew me away? I've seen people quit affiliate marketing after losing $150. However, these are the same people who owe $ 50,000 for a college degree and still don't have a job. Affiliate marketing is low risk when compared to starting a real business. Think how much debt people have to incur to start a restaurant (and they have a default rate of 60% after 3 years).

4. How Much Money Can Affiliate Marketers Make?

This is like asking a business owner, "How much can you earn to start a business?" I've had days in the past when I've made more than $ 100,000 in profit in one day. But that is not common.

This corresponds to 1% of the 1% during the boom phase. There are so many factors that determine how much an affiliate marketer can earn. I would say the average full-time partner can make $ 5,000 to $ 20,000 a month.

A "super partner" is someone who can make more than $ 1.5 million in profit per year.

5. How long does it take to be successful?

There are too many factors to give a definitive answer. However, in my observations, it usually takes a few months to two years for the typical partner to be successful (if they dedicate themselves to it every day).

These are the main factors that will affect your success rate.

How much money can you invest? The more you can invest, the better. More money means better tools. More money means you can attend conferences and network. More money means you can collect more data for your campaigns.

What skills and experience do you already have (copywriting, design, programming)? You can always outsource design and programming, but I recommend that you understand how to write copy.

Do people help you? I'm not saying you should be spending money on a mentor. Are there meetings with local partners in your city? See if you can find someone there who can help you. Can you connect with someone on forums?

How much time are you willing to invest? I know that you are busy. We are all busy. But the fact is, there are now people out there who are much busier than you, who made it work. I didn't have a lot of time when I started, but I took my time. I spent 1.5 hours a day in traffic in Atlanta. I moved to an apartment that was within walking distance of my 9 to 5 job to save 70 minutes a day. I've given up a lot of my personal life. On weekends, I would stop partying, going on dates, and playing video games. Every free time I had was devoted to affiliate marketing.

One word of warning, my greatest regret is that I have neglected my health in the process. I didn't sleep much, I had a poor diet, and I didn't exercise. That goes backwards. If I had focused more on my health, I would have had more energy to work on my campaigns.

I don't promise you'll be a millionaire in a few months or anything. It will take time. I had to sacrifice a few months. But because of that, I live a life that very few people can live. I think it's harder to be broke for a few decades.

6. How much do you want it?

I've seen too many people "trying" affiliate marketing. It's like people who go to the gym at the beginning of the year and leave after a few weeks. Thousands of people will take this course.

Most will not finish it completely or complete one of the tasks due to laziness. This guide is not for these people. This book is for 3% who really want to be successful. It is not for beginners.

7. Do I have to incur credit card debt for affiliate marketing to work?

Don't spend money you don't have. This is the sign of someone who is impatient.

That happened to my friend a few years ago. He had a burning desire to be successful in affiliate marketing, but he didn't have the money to fund affiliate marketing campaigns. He decided to write everything on his credit card because he was so sure he would do it.

What happened? He was in debt to the value of $ 10,000 and did not have a profitable campaign. This is not "investing" ... this is gambling.

I know you are in a hurry to be successful, but you must learn to be patient. Grab a few part-time jobs and get to work. Credit cards should only be used when you have profitable campaigns and need the extra cash flow.

8. Do I have to be dodgy to make money from affiliate marketing?

Affiliate marketing doesn't have the best reputation. Some partners promote products that are shady, such as: B. Diet pills. Others make misleading promises in their ads to make sales.

Affiliate marketing is just one industry. What you promote and how you promote it is 100% up to you. Are there dodgy affiliate marketers? Absolutely. But would it be seedy to recommend a product you like on Amazon? Not really.

The good news is that there are many ways to make money from 100% legitimate affiliate marketing such as: B. lead generation, e-commerce, game / app advertising, etc.

Key Takeaways:

It's not too late to start in affiliate marketing

No one can predict how long it'll take for you to become successful. It's dependent on you.

Don't spend money you don't have on affiliate marketing. Be patient.

CHAPTER TWO

MINDSET TO BE SUCCESSFUL WITH AFFILIATE MARKETING

You cannot succeed in this industry if you have a weak mindset. I've seen so many people who could have been successful in this area.

They had the technical skills

They had the money to invest

They had the connections and mentors

They had the work ethic

What was the missing ingredient? They had a weak mentality. They were soft! I've seen so many examples of this in sports where the superior team or player should have won the championship, but they couldn't handle the pressure. There wasn't a connection.

They didn't have that mamba mentality. This also applies to affiliate marketing. All of the world's campaign strategies and tactics don't matter if you quit because you have a lot of money.

I know you are excited and motivated now, but will you still be motivated in 6 months? Or if you've lost money trying to find out? I had no natural talents when I started at the age of 23. I would say the odds were against me when I started.

Although I went to Georgia Tech, I did not graduate with honors

I ended up in debt up to around $ 20,000. I barely had the money to run campaigns.

I didn't know anyone in the industry at all. I had no mentors and I couldn't afford lessons. I only had forums.

I didn't know how to program. I still don't know!

Despite all my weaknesses, I had strength. It was my murderous attitude. My grit. My attitude of never giving up. The good news is that mindsets can be learned, and I'll show you the main ones.

Mindset # 1: If you want to be successful faster, you will fail twice as fast.

Brazilian Jiu Jitsu is one of my hobbies. My coaches are ready to teach me everything they know. I can pay for lessons. I can buy books and videos to learn from different champions. The blueprint for success is increasingly going to class and exercising more.

If you want to get good at chess, there are an unlimited number of resources you can learn from. With affiliate marketing, no one

26

is going to tell you everything. I'll give you the basics, but you'll have to figure out the rest.

This kills a lot of people because they are used to learning from textbooks. They don't understand that this is discovery learning. This is not an industry where you can learn only by studying. You learn by doing your own experiments as if you were a scientist. Making money with a campaign is a skill. And as with all skills, it takes practice.

Start a campaign. Learn from it; and repeat. "Your first 10,000 photos are your worst," said a famous photographer. This is how it works with affiliate marketing. Your first campaigns are worthless and lose money. But everyone who has been successful in this industry has seen this point.

The mindset that has helped me the most is failing twice as quickly. Failure is something that needs to be embraced, not avoided. You have taken action and tested a hypothesis. It doesn't work, now find another way.

Mindset 2: It only takes one campaign

Nobody counts how many times you've failed. I started in 2008. I spent 6 months, lost $ 5,000, failed 15 campaigns before finally finding my winner. This first successful campaign is the catalyst and a turning point for your success.

Where would I be today if I finished Campaign # 14? I would be pigeonholed now and hate my life. When you want to give up, imagine you are one campaign away from anything you want.

Mindset # 3: Overcome your fear of losing money

Losing money is worthless. There is no sugar coating. In affiliate marketing, you can lose hundreds or even thousands of dollars before launching your first profitable campaign.

You have to invest in servers, tracking software, and money to pay for the traffic. And I understand the pain and fear of losing money. It is natural. There is a psychological principle called loss aversion. It hurts more to lose $ 100 than it feels good to make $ 200. We are programmed to avoid risks.

How do we overcome this belief? When I lose $ 200, I don't think about the lost opportunity. I don't think I could have used the money for fine dining or gadgets. The $ 200 is an investment in my future. I don't get emotional. That $ 200 is for me to buy data. I am a scientist doing marketing experiments. I thought $ 200 would be gone before I even put it into campaigns.

Do you know what I think is strange? It is acceptable to go into huge debt to pay off school. I know people who owe more than $ 100,000 and don't even have jobs.

Society accepts this risk-benefit ratio. But are you losing a few hundred dollars to test affiliate marketing campaigns? Everyone is losing their mind! Don't think of it as a loss of money. You invest in your company.

Mindset # 4: Be patient

I've lost hundreds of dollars with each campaign. And it felt like all the split tests I was working on didn't matter. I then read about the Chinese history of bamboo. Nothing happens in the first years of a bamboo tree's growth. You water it, but you don't see many results.

After a few years, it can grow up to 80 feet in one year. You couldn't see the results, but it was making progress. In order for the tree to grow, it must spend time developing its roots. That's what happened to my campaigns.

A campaign was not profitable, but I learned how to do my first quote tests. I was not profitable in another campaign, but started my first international campaign. I lost $ 200 in another campaign, but found that landing pages work. It wasn't until my 14th campaign that everything exploded. That campaign put all the pieces of the puzzle together. Every action you take is the seed of success. You just don't know where the fruit will grow.

Mindset # 5: Burn the ships

Hernán Cortés landed in Mexico in the early 16th century. He was on a mission from Spain to find gold. He only had 600 men. The task? Conquer the Aztec Empire. In the middle of the night he sent one of his men to set his ships on fire. You can imagine how the men felt. They wanted his head on a stick. But he said "Now there is no plan B. You won't be able to return to Spain now". It was either death or victory.

I've seen too many people "try" affiliate marketing. Do you know how many people see my "writing" on Facebook and ask me for help? 95% of them don't even start their first campaigns.

Me? I was ready to die for it. To my way of thinking, I didn't have a plan B. I didn't do anything but affiliate marketing. If you say this halfway then how can you compete with someone who is giving it 100%?

All of my money, energy, and time literally went into affiliate marketing. Yes, I had to bring some, but now, it's easy to say it was worth it.

Main learning points:

It doesn't matter how often you fail. It only takes one campaign to change your life.

Burn the ships. You have to go all-in if you are to be successful.

Don't get emotional when campaigns fail. You are a scientist collecting data.

CHAPTER THREE

HOW TO PICK UP YOUR NICHE

Choosing the right niche for the affiliate market is not a choice for everyone. Each person has different strengths and depending on their own abilities, they must take these elements into account.

Finding a niche is one of the most daunting steps of the affiliate marketer's journey. But it is a step that cannot be overlooked or rushed. Finding the right niche is key to tapping into a strong buyer's market that isn't saturated with competition.

Some seasoned affiliate marketers say you don't have to stick to familiar content - suggesting you can explore one of the niches in affiliate marketing - and while it's true, the learning curve can be long in some of those potential niches. Since most of these niches are generally very competitive, it may be worthwhile to pick an initial topic that you have experience and knowledge of.

Choosing The Best Niches for Affiliate Marketing

The ideal situation, of course, is to find an area with little competition. There are tools like Google Keyword Planner, SEMRush and SpyFu that show volume and level of competition to give some insight. While competition will continue to be higher and lower in the purchase funnel, the conditions for a large amount of traffic - whether organic or through paid and other traffic sources – they should not necessarily be overlooked as a potential opportunity. However, there are many subcategories of these evergreen niches that can be a solid starting point for those new to affiliate marketing.

These smaller areas allow partners to build a brand on these more specific topics and gradually move on to the broader ones. As Rae Dolan, a well-known affiliate marketer, says:

"Almost every broad niche has multiple subdivisions that can offer you an opportunity. Even so, I would make sure that the domain and brand you are working with is able to expand to broader content and monetization opportunities as your brand grows."

Her steps in choosing a niche includes points every partner should use in making their decision:

Use PPC bids as an indicator of competition and interest in the subject. If no one is advertising in the room, or if the volume and bids are low, it could be an indication of limited appeal.

By searching for the keywords in your niche, you can tell if all of the results are big brand home pages, indicating high competition. If they have small blogs or deep pages on the first page, you may have a chance, and have done some of your initial keyword research.

When you have your list of ranking websites, check their inbound links to see how difficult it will be to match the numbers.

Connected Niche Audience

When choosing your target audience, a few other factors can be used to make the process easier. When you are part of the audience you want to reach, it is easier to choose terms and understand the questions similar people will have. The topic may also be one that you are curious about, so the research interests you and the learning curve is not that steep.

Once you are in the area, ask questions to answer any issues or concerns you may find in the area. People are looking for answers. So knowing what they're asking can help with smart content that captures interest and placements. Aside from looking at the suggested searches when you start typing in the Google search box, there are forums and platforms that can also be used to find questions in the niche.

Learning and understanding the terminology can also be an important factor in choosing a profitable niche. When language and terminology are unclear, definitions and explanations can be solid content that people often search for. Using the right words is important not only in creating content and potential paid traffic options, but also in including them in ad copies and landing pages to attract people into the niche.

Competition in Your Affiliate Niche

A number of other factors can be used to facilitate the process when choosing your target audience. Being part of the target audience you want to reach will make it easier to choose terms and understand the questions similar people will have. The topic may also be one that you are curious about, so the research interests you and the learning curve is not that steep.

Once you have a list of potential topics and popular niche markets, be sure to check out what partners have to offer in that space. If you are looking for web development or want to create an online presence, finding affiliate advertisers in this area is your next step. Domain registration, hosting and SSL certificates (and yes, all the products Namecheap Affiliate Marketing offers) are areas where payment and conversion potential needs to be checked and considered. You should test your traffic to see if the provider with the highest commission is actually converting better than others with lower commissions. A higher conversion can be the result of a lower price, lower brand popularity, or better reviews.

This deliberation and testing of margins and success is critical and should be researched and tested with as much effort as is expended in selecting keywords and niches.

High quality products tend to pay higher commissions, but they are also lower in volume and typically lower in income. These types of factors should be studied before making a final decision. You can also check the availability of a suitable domain name for the niche. If finding a clear, relevant domain is difficult, this can be a competitive partner to build a presence with.

You should also look for a supplier who has solid support for their partners. An advertiser who tracks and interacts with their partners can help you choose where to market your website. A provider who produces regularly updated ads and provides solid resources and support will make your job easier.

There are a number of websites out there that follow the cutting edge topics for affiliate marketers. Viper Chill posts generally contain solid affiliate marketing content.

How to Discover The Best Affiliate Marketing Niches in 2021

The most profitable niches in affiliate marketing are those with ever-green demand, those with avid fans, or both.

If you're investing time, money, and effort in building an affiliate site, it makes sense to ask ahead of time if the niche itself might be profitable in the long run.

You can make money in the short term doing what's trending right now, but decades of profit include more mundane things like: Golf.

What are the most profitable affiliate marketing niches?

Here's our shortlist of the niches most likely to make big bucks:

Hobby niches - photography, travel, sports betting, event tickets, casino

Niches of money - debt settlement, bitcoin, investing, credit card, mortgage

Health and fitness niches - Weight loss, fitness, yoga, organic produce, diet, e.g vegan

Lifestyle niches - luxury, cruises, travel, online dating, airlines, fashion, jewelry

Home and family niches - home security, coffee, baby products, dogs, gardening

Tech Niches - web hosting, WordPress, VPN, SaaS, gaming, software

Alternative niches - CBD, marijuana, essential oils, herbs, personal development

Now that we've given you the TLDR version, let's take a look at the full list of the - in our humble opinion - affiliate marketing niches. It's a lot of work figuring out which niche to build a site in. In fact, this is where most new partners stop - yes, even before posting their first message.

Sometimes it seems like you have better luck finding a unicorn. But what if I told you these unicorn affiliate marketing niches exist? And that we share them with you, plus at least 6 profitable affiliate programs for every niche.

Programs that are statistically proven to make money. Get ready to take lots of notes as I will be giving you a lot of tips and guidance.

List of The 60+ Best Affiliate Marketing Niches

1. Golf

This is probably no surprise to someone who has been in the affiliate marketing game for over a few months, but golf is one of those hugely lucrative markets (you will find that most of the luxury markets are profitable affiliate niche markets).

In fact, the global golf industry is valued at $ 12.55 billion a year. Each year.

The average golfer spends approximately £ 214 ($ 275) per month or £ 2,568 ($ 3,305) per year on his hobby.

While it may seem like an elite pastime, it is played by people from all walks of life.

And they all have one very common trait: they like to spend what they can afford to improve their game.

Yes, golf can be a competitive niche, but I was still able to find 149,000 phrases with a KD of no more than 20 in Ahrefs, making it one of the best niches for affiliate marketing in 2021.

It's also pretty easy to get familiar with free tips and training content. The demand for technical knowledge is there and most websites are not particularly successful.

2. Home security

I have never taken home security that seriously until recently. That changed, however, when my house was broken into a little over two years ago. Having your home broken into is a very difficult experience.

Home security immediately became a priority for me because my girlfriend was afraid of falling asleep at night.

I have invested in new internal and external locks, window security locks, Wi-Fi cameras, external motion sensor lights, and a monitored home alarm system with multiple internal sensors.

Basically, I dropped the best part of a wing to make sure she felt safe again. And that's one of the things that make affiliate marketing great niches: the sense of urgency. In the US, 1.24 million households are broken into every year. So this is a laser-focused audience that needs your help.

3. Online dating

It's funny how far the online dating industry has come in the past two decades. There is a niche for affiliate marketing that has been there to begin with.

Once upon a time, someone who found a partner on an online dating website was thought of as a little ... well ... weird. Times have changed, however, and online dating isn't just acceptable - it's cool!

How Much is the Dating Industry Really Worth? The latest estimate is that it is expected to reach $ 2 billion per year with an annual growth of 6% for the foreseeable future. The same data also shows that at least 24% of people use or have used online dating sites in the past.

The reason this industry has become so profitable is because whatever people believe, humans are social animals. We long to be part of a tribe and then start our own tribe in time. Helping single men and women achieve that original life goal can be one of the most lucrative niches to partner with if you know the best programs that can be funded.

4. Travel

There's a big old world out there, and the abundance of cheap flights means you can visit even the most remote coasts without winning the lottery. Okay, you may have to travel economy class and give up the luxury of business class, but that's a small price to pay.

People travel today more than ever in human history. This is bad news for governments fearful of pandemics. But it's very good news for the travel industry, which gets its hands on an estimated $ 7 trillion (yes, with a 't') annually

That said, it's one of the biggest affiliate niches out there, and there are plenty of lucrative programs out there to help you with that.

Travel spans a variety of potential niches and sub-niches, from the usual hotels and flights to city tours, luggage, insurance, and even clothing. So you don't have to take the same persistent approach that most member airlines do; Try to swing cheap flights and hotels.

5. Gaming

Good to know: I built my first PC so I could play X-Wing on it ... under MS-DOS. No you are old! Gaming has always been a part of my life, so it was cool to see how it moved on with every decade.

The gaming audience has now expanded to include not only consoles but also mobile devices. And mobile is big in the networked industry. About 200 million people play video games in North America alone, but that's a drop in the ocean compared to the estimated 2.5 billion players worldwide.

Gaming is a niche similar to golf in that the average gamer is happy to drop hundreds of dollars on a new GPU or gaming chair. And repeat this process every year.

There is almost a luxury segment with endless demand in this market. The gaming niche is generally one of the more competitive niches for affiliate marketing. but I was still able to find 25,919 keywords with a KD of no more than 20. Also, there are several gaming niches I can work with and an ever increasing demand in this category.

6. Home Décor

Home decor is one of those evergreen niches worth a serious look. Why?

Well, because people decorate their homes to sell or renovate a house or apartment they've just bought. People spend an average of between $ 500 and $ 5,000 decorating or renovating every room in their home.

What about recessions?

It's the same business, but to a lesser extent - walls need to be painted, sofas replaced, etc. But homeowners will want to do it as cheaply as possible during a recession, that's a niche in itself (but I like the luxury segment too).

This affiliate niche also has deals that pay between $ 100 and $ 200 per sale, depending on the product category. Really.

7. Financial

Yes, we actually name the financial niche as profitable because it is natural.

We've also included it here because most new affiliate marketers stay away from it because they assume it's a saturated niche. It's competitive, but it's also a lot easier than, say, making money from adult content.

In our article on Successful Affiliate Marketing Websites, you can see some examples of affiliate companies making serious money in this niche. You are proof that you really just need a unique point of view and are ready to work hard.

In short, people are going into more debt than ever before. So there is a huge market for the products and services that we have identified for you. So if you can make it work, it's one of the best affiliate marketing niches, but you should be a veteran if you consider this category.

8. Cruises

Growing up, I always thought that only really rich people went on cruises. And maybe that was once true, but it isn't anymore.

Here's a chew stat - somewhere in the region of 26 million people go on cruises every year. The same people in the region will spend $ 3,600 per capita on their vacations at sea. It all adds up to an industry worth about $ 125 billion a year.

People from all walks of life take cruises, and there are cruises that cater for everything from singles to rock music fans. One tip is to find a sub-niche in this and / or focus on the thousands of informational keywords that have very low KD scores. This can be a very lucrative niche with the right approach.

9. Fitness

This is another one of those evergreen niches that you can be 99% sure will be available in about 50 years. That's because the fitness industry has been going, give or take, for about 4,000 years.

Most of the ancient empires insisted that young men be trained physically, usually for battle, but you should also consider the first ancient Olympics about 2,700 years ago.

In any case, the point we're making here is that getting and staying fit has always been part of a healthy life. This is also why the fitness industry is worth $ 3.7 trillion a year as a whole.

The really good news is that there is a lot of money to be made from an online business by going the less traveled route in this affiliate niche.

10. Music

Millions of potential new musicians are born every year, and by the time they are six years old, 28% of them will study a musical instrument.

For 14-year-olds this rises to over 40%. And that without taking into account the growing number of people who start playing musical instruments much later in life. What we are striving for here is that many people play or want to play musical instruments.

All you have to do is make them offers that they will happily pay for. But that's the problem with the music niche: in fact, profitable programs are hard to come by. So that's what we did, and some of these programs offer up to $ 35 per sale.

I also like this niche because it is one of those niches in affiliate marketing that is always green and you can create small websites that will make money for years and give you the real passive income that you are looking for in internet marketing . There are many ideas for small niche websites to brainstorm this broad niche.

11. Weight Loss

Helping people lose weight can be one of the best ways to make money online. Especially when you consider that a staggering percentage of children and adults are now classified as pathologically obese.

In short, people know deep down that obesity is not healthy. And that's why so many people are looking for ways to shed those pounds with an easy-to-follow diet. But remember, most of the people in these niches are now skeptical of diets and beverages that promise magical weight loss numbers.

Instead, they seek a weight loss program and keep it off. This means that you can combine the research from this niche with the data from the fitness niche above. In any case, consumers in this category spend $ 60 billion every year to lose weight.

12. Real estate

There is a limited amount of habitable land on our planet. A finite commodity has a higher market value, i.e. real estate is never devalued to zero. Yes, recessions and depression can occur and devalue them.

But - almost without exception - house prices are at least recovering to pre-recession levels. Somewhere in the region of 5 million houses change hands every year in a market worth nearly $ 30 trillion. So there is always a demand.

The money to be made here is in sub-niches, like the FSBO craze a decade ago or the luxury segment or other niche markets.

In short, there is little point in trying to compete with Zillow or Trulia in their own category. However, you can focus on the thousands of informational questions (like, what is, etc.) with surprisingly low KD values for such competitive markets.

13. Debt settlement

A large number of people have a lot of debts that they can't pay off or write off. For example, there is currently $ 829 billion in credit card debt in the United States.

Most people hate the idea of being in debt and are constantly looking for solutions to it. And wherever you find problem / solution scenarios, I can guarantee you will find the opportunity to make money online in various sub-niche debt settlement markets.

In this case, it is done through debt consolidation, credit score, and social finance offers. In this niche, there are affiliate programs with payouts of $ 50, $ 100, and $ 150 per lead.

14. Sports

Ah, sports fans - people who are willing to part with unhealthy amounts to enjoy their hobby. Sometimes it is just as a spectator and not as a participant. There's nothing wrong with that, especially from a partner's point of view.

But we know it will be difficult to make serious money selling jockstraps and shoelaces. That's why we've put together some really cool affiliate sports programs for you, including all the common stuff like clothing and exercise equipment for various niche sports markets. And also some very cool sports memorabilia, drinking services, and affiliate programs. All of these can result in healthy profits for your business as an affiliate marketer.

15. Yoga

It wasn't long ago that anyone who wanted to study real yoga had to pack their bags and travel to an ashram in India. Today, the demand is so high that you can find multiple yoga schools in any city or major city.

Yoga is more popular than ever as people are looking for a way to relax and find a little inner peace by exercising to supplement their diet. Your job is to connect them to products and services that will enhance their yoga experience.

16. Airlines

We're big fans of evaluating a niche before investing your time and money building a page of authority around it. When we researched the aviation industry, this piqued our interest. And we were absolutely amazed!!!!!

Did you know that in the US alone, $ 2.1 million per minute is spent on air travel?

Air travel has gotten much cheaper, so people do this more often for both personal and business reasons. Note, however, that the profit margins in this industry are paper thin. This means that there are a lot of affiliate commissions to be paid, but they amount to around $ 25 per sale.

17. Coffee

Did you know that the average person drinks at least 3 cups of coffee every day?

That will cost them $ 9 a day or $ 180 a month. But that's exactly what they spend on their 9-5 coffee. You could almost say that coffee is a luxury right now.

When you consider that they might have a coffee grinder and / or percolator to use at home and order specialty coffee blends, you will understand why the US coffee category is valued at nearly $ 75 billion a year.

Coffee is only part of our daily diet, and people can be quite passionate about it. Or crazy, depending on how long it has been since they ran out of caffeine.

18. Make-up

One of the real tricks to making money online is finding a niche that stays golden through good times and bad. A niche where people spend money, even when they are really broke.

Cosmetics / beauty is a perfect example of this kind of niche - sales are increasing even during an economic downturn. Why?

Because the average person wants to feel good about the way they look, especially if they can't afford to do anything else.

People are going to spend money on this, even when they are broke.

Now you could easily say that people buy make-up locally, so there is little point in advertising it online.

19. Photography

You may think you don't know enough about photography to run an affiliate site on the subject. Most photographers are amateurs or hobbyists.

So you don't have to be an award-winning photographer to have a voice in this niche. And the second is that a number of bloggers have built an entire affiliate marketing business around their photo blogs. Don't believe us? Google a guy named Joshua Dunlop.

Another benefit of operating in this niche is that photographers don't even think twice about putting hundreds of dollars on a new camera.

20. Supplements

You might have noticed a little trend in the niches we mentioned so far?

Note: some of them are related in one form or another to health and nutrition or luxury. And the insert sheet is just another example of this.

The stereotype of a supplement user is that someone is drinking protein shakes. But this niche is far more nuanced than this, especially when it comes to nootropics, or what people call "smart drugs."

In short, this industry is currently valued at at least $ 120 billion a year and will double in a decade. And let's not forget that there are also pet food supplements that are doubling the market again.

21. Insurance

Selling insurance is an odd niche if you think about it - you're selling someone financial protection against something that could happen. But if the worst doesn't happen, the insurance company will withdraw the profit.

This also explains why the North American insurance industry is worth $ 1.2 trillion a year. But people are happy to pay the premiums because the average cost of even a small car accident is around $ 7,500.

The nice thing about the insurance niche is that you can break it down into sub-categories like auto, homeowner, health, life, travel, pets, etc. There is even volcano insurance. Yes it is real

All you have to do is think a little sideways to introduce an affiliate insurance program to an existing audience.

22. Jewelry

This niche is a no-brainer. People love to buy jewelry, jewelry costs money, so there is money to be made.

In fact, consumers from all walks of life spend an average of $ 300 billion per year on watches, rings, bracelets, etc. And that's the main point that needs to be emphasized here: jewelry isn't just for the "rich" people. Bling makes people feel good.

Now, most jewelry is bought as a gift for someone else, but about 30% of all jewelry sold internationally comes from online sales by affiliates. Although there are jewelry stores in almost every city, people still choose to shop online. Imagine that.

This is good news for you, especially considering that there are offers that pay out an average commission of $ 900 per sale. This is not a typo.

23. Auto

Some niches may not make your heart beat faster, however, if you're a bit of a car enthusiast, this is the perfect niche for you - it combines something important to you with the opportunity to earn a full-time income from related programs.

The offers are quite varied, ranging from motorcycles and muscle cars to golf carts.

24. Baby products

If you're not sure if the baby niche is right for you, here are some things to keep in mind: By the time you read this, 20 children have been born.

Don't believe us? Take a look at the world population clock and you will see that this is a growing market.

That, plus the fact that most new parents will spend about $ 10,000 in their first year of life, taking care of their new baby.

How many niches can you imagine where people have a moral obligation to spend money on? I agree.

25. Bitcoin and cryptos

I sincerely admire how cryptocurrencies have contributed to the disruption of the FIAT currency markets. Because they had to be disturbed.

And even though you have all seen Bitcoin rise and then falter completely, cryptocurrencies are here to stay.

Bitcoin, for example, has seen quite an impressive rebound in the last 6 months.

This means that the "enthusiasm" is far from over. So you are still an early adopter if you reach this niche as soon as possible.

26. Casino

But ... but isn't the casino industry just insane and incredibly competitive?

Yes and no. Yes, it can be difficult to get back links to gambling sites. But "no", this niche is not as competitive as people say.

We found 38,131 long-tail keywords in Ahrefs with a KD score of 10 or less and an additional 768 "questions" with a KD score of 10 or less. That's only an example. And then you have to remember that gambling has literally always existed, probably since the first caveman growled, "I bet Thrakk can't escape the tigers with huge teeth out there."

27. CBD

I don't think anyone would have expected cannabis to be made as quickly or to the extent that it is legal.

Now, CBD-based products aren't quite the same as they lack the THC (tetrahydrocannabinol) component that makes you high.

Instead, the CBD industry is focusing on the health benefits that humans and animals can get from ingesting cannabidiol products.

For example, it seems to have pretty much cured my dog's arthritis - this is not medical advice, just my personal experience. Because we don't want to be prosecuted, do we?

The CBD industry is valued at around $ 18 billion at the time of writing, with steady growth projected for at least the next decade.

28. Christian

If you've read anything by Sam Harris, Christopher Hitchens, or Richard Dawkins, it's easy to assume that the Christian faith is in decline.

The opposite is the case: many people who were once atheists are rethinking their options, so to speak.

There are currently 2.4 billion Christians on this planet, so you can open up a huge market. But what on earth could you sell to Christians?

How about movie streaming services, gifts, home decor, clothing, and even crafts with a Christian touch?

29. Invest

Relax, you don't have to be a Warren Buffet to post content in the investment niche.

In fact, the majority of investors are relatively new and looking for advice on how to get started.

That's because most people haven't invested or saved anything for retirement - they need a solution to their problem.

We've found some really nice investment partner deals for you, including the usual stuff like stock portfolios, as well as real estate, precious metals and peer-to-peer crypto loans. And some of them pay up to $ 70 per lead.

30. Luxury

This is a niche in itself, but it is also a great way to identify sub or tangent niches.

So if you have a blog or website that caters to a rich audience, these programs are ideal for you. However, this list of affiliate offers is also helpful for anyone struggling to find a niche. One that's not quite mainstream, but certainly lucrative.

Like mattresses that pay more than $ 300 per sale or private jet rental companies that pay more than $ 3,000 per lead. And that's just a random selection of what you'll find in the list.

31. Organic products

The "green" industry is estimated at $ 4 trillion per year.

That number includes everything from solar energy to recycled toilet paper. People are willing to spend money to improve their environmental awareness.

Currently, the "green" movement is more of an "avid fan" than it has been since the 1970s. That makes it perfect for advertising organic products.

That doesn't mean you sell quinoa to them by mail order, however. There are many more exciting things for you including beauty products.

32. Pet

I am a dog owner so I know how happy other pet owners are to take care of their furry friends. (Well, my dog adopted me, but that's a whole different story about what's really important in life.)

In my case it was thousands of Euros, including two surgeries, just for her health. And that explains why the U.S. pet market is valued at at least $ 70 billion a year.

Imagine the amount of what the international market is worth. This can be viewed as a competitive niche, but there is still a lot of market for new affiliate publishers with a passion for pets.

33. Solar energy

A friend of mine recently went 100% off the grid and no longer has to pay for electricity. I've been almost obsessed with this idea since he told me.

That is why I am working to implement as much solar energy as possible in my own home. I'm not alone either, the solar industry is estimated to be around $ 400 billion a year.

You can advertise everything from solar chargers for mobile devices to complete solar power systems for the home.

34. Vegan

I'm not and never will be a vegan, but it's hard to ignore the implications of those words: "A country's greatness and moral progress can be measured by the way its animals are treated." Gandhi

Vegetarianism has been around for a long time, but veganism has only been a lifestyle choice since the 19th century. There is a big push towards veganism to prevent the climate change that you have learned about through social media. Because of this, the United States has six times as many vegans as it did ten years ago.

The plant-based food industry is expected to be worth more than $ 20 billion over the next decade. In the vegan niche market, however, there is much more to promote than just groceries - such as beauty products, dietary supplements and much more.

35. Diet

And we're closing our collection of affiliate niches with another "healthy" niche: nutrition. As part of the really massive health and wellness industry, nutrition is valued at $ 700 billion.

There is a clear trend that people are much more aware of the foods they are eating. People are now ready to spend more if it allows them to eat healthier, more nutritious foods.

This applies to both restaurants and private households. Hence, this market remains open to the many subscription companies that serve them. And they are only the tip of the iceberg in terms of the offers and programs that you can promote.

36. Marijuana

You need to know how much affiliate marketing can change in a few years.

For example, how marijuana affiliate programs are a thing now. And a very profitable business - you see a market worth $ 63 billion.

The programs listed include everything from accessories and supplies such as vaporizers, tents and soil, to the different types of seeds you can sow.

Cannabis is legal in various states of the Union and in countries around the world. This is certainly a growth market. This is the worst word game ever.

Seriously, if you're an early adopter here, you can make money for retirement faster than almost any other niche.

37. Personal development

We all want to be the best possible version of ourselves.

Who wouldn't want to be smarter, stronger, less distracted, more peaceful, richer, or better, or just have more free time? Maybe not all at once, but I'm sure you can relate to at least one of the above goals as a personal goal ... that you haven't reached yet.

In fact, we know we can do better ... and we want to. Because of this, the personal development niche is estimated at an estimated $ 13 billion per year.

People like to invest money in a workable personal development program. All you need to do is match them with the best you can find.

38. Essential oils

Here's a somewhat tangential health niche that you probably didn't think was cash-in, or assumed was absolutely saturated. Not so.

In fact, the essential oils niche is currently experiencing both strong growth and increasing popularity.

A lot has to do with people looking for alternative ways to manage their health problems. As a result, the market is expected to double to at least $ 27 billion in the coming years.

That makes it 3x more valuable than the online dating niche. And there are literally thousands of low competition keywords waiting to be won.

Thousands. And no, none of the affiliate programs listed has anything to do with the nasty MLM business plans you've heard of.

Only the types of products and services that you want to post on your blog.

39. Vaping

At least 500,000 people die from smoking-related diseases in the United States each year.

Smoking cigarettes has been proven bad for you and that comes from a smoker. Yes, yes, it's a dirty habit and I am ashamed of myself.

However, if you focus on why you should consider this niche, you will find that there are reasons that $ 19.3 billion is accurate.

More people are buying vapes than ever before - the market has tripled in the past five years. And if anything, regulating vaping will legitimize it and encourage more people to try it at least for the first time.

Regardless of what the mainstream media is complaining about, vaping isn't going to go away anytime soon. The numbers don't support the hysteria.

40. Dogs

People tend to think dogs are just cute. And they are - we love our dogs, right? But our relationship with dogs is much more complex.

Did you know that dogs release oxytocin (the substance of love) when you look at them or pet them, and that your cortisol (stress hormone) levels drop when you hang out with your furry friend? So there is no doubt that dogs are good for your health.

No wonder, then, that dog owners spend an average of $ 1,200 a year on feeding, grooming, and caring for their prized dog.

Are you worried it is already saturated? It isn't - there are tens of thousands of low comp keywords you can use to post content.

41. Restaurant

Have you never seen restaurants as a potential niche until you read this? You are not alone in this.

This is one of those surprising niches that I've found in terms of the programs we've found and how much money some of them pay to partners. In the US alone, the restaurant supply industry is estimated to be worth $ 44 billion a year - that's just groceries, plates, forks, knives, and utensils.

Yes, some programs are of the Dinner Certificate type, but we've also discovered some really new products and services.

42. Sports betting

Before we go any further, there is one thing we need to be clear: sports betting is a very competitive industry.

To call it a killer is actually an understatement. But it can also be insanely profitable - doing 6 songs a month can be the norm for many super partners.

While we understand that some affiliate marketers may question access to this niche for moral or ethical reasons, I have a double question for you:

When was the last time you bought a lottery ticket and how is that different from wagering $ 5 on your favorite team to win?

The reality is that people are betting online whether you agree or not. With a market value of $ 225 billion per year, a lot of money can be made here.

43. Fish

One of my earliest memories is when my father taught me to throw sand out of the damp sand of a beach town near where I now live. On a hot summer day, I smell the salt from the same stretch of sea. For him it was a father-son tradition, but also a skill that can be used later in life.

So I lived this: "... teach a man to fish and he can make a living all his life." And every year 49 million Americans practice this skill for the same reasons.

Fishing itself takes many forms, from sport to recreation, but total recreational fishing is estimated at $ 212 billion a year.

44. Education

You are probably wondering how to make money from education? The first is promoting online educational programs and exam guides.

The internet began as a learning resource for schools and colleges before we hijacked it to share adorable cat photos and memes.

However, the nice thing about the internet is that it still makes the educational process easier - you can get a degree even if you live on top of a mountain. And then you can add other physical aspects of the work like paper, pens, chairs, desks, etc.

See, this is how you monetize education ... once you have the right affiliate programs to promote them.

45. Books

I remember talking to one of my sisters about how insecure she was about owning a Kindle. That it could somehow help bring about the end of paper books.

But I replied that I thought a percentage of readers would always wish their favorite book to be at hand. Apparently I was right ... without predicting the explosive growth of the Kindle market.

The print book industry is still valued at $ 119 billion a year, and there is a thriving market for used book sales - both as buyers and sellers. And with a different twist, there is also a new sub-niche: eTextbook rental for students.

So now is a great time to start an affiliate site on any of the above topics.

46. Tickets to events

Choose an affiliate marketer and ask them to come up with ideas for a new affiliate site. Event tickets may not appear on the radar or may be discounted.

While that is understandable, it would also mean missing out on an industry where consumers are spending at least $ 60 billion and $ 80 billion this year before it's time to elect a new president. This consists of tickets for events, attractions in certain cities or just certain attractions.

The point is that people of all ages and walks of life book their event tickets online.

47. Herbs

When you think of sage, lavender, or thyme, you don't automatically think of something that can make you rich. But in the past these herbs were worth their weight in gold.

In fact, saffron is still worth the same as gold - $ 5,040 a pound to be precise.

While we cannot promise such revenues, we were a little baffled to find that the herbal medicine industry is worth more than $ 70 billion a year.

48. Gob

A long time ago there was the idea of having a job for life. Nowadays the average worker has several jobs and / or careers in his life.

That's the norm now. And the market will change drastically again once automation becomes mainstream for jobs in the service sector. We're talking maybe 25 years later.

But right now, people looking for a new job need help with everything from their resume to learning new skills, preparing for their interview, to getting dressed. And yes, I've found affiliate programs for you in each of these sub-company programs, even with enviable commission rates.

49. VPN

There has never been a better market for VPNs than now. And if there was justice in the world, Edward Snowden would get a slice of every VPN package sold.

He revealed what people have long suspected: that our governments are actively seeking private data. That made virtual private networks all the rage for nerds and geeks in an industry with annual sales of $ 50 billion.

So you can help your visitors browse the web anonymously while protecting themselves from identity theft and other online security threats, or even give them access to the entire library of their favorite online media streaming service. Regardless, this is a growth industry with the potential for a lot of affiliate revenue.

50. Pharmaceuticals

Relax, we know the kind of images that "Pharma" affiliate programs evoke in most people. However, this summary has nothing to do with such products.

Instead, we've tracked down legitimate programs that cover everything from mail-order prescriptions to drug discount programs to drugstore networks. So it is nothing more than the other "research" posts.

Is this niche worth your time and effort? Well, it is worth $ 128 billion a year. So that's a resounding "yes".

51. Gardening

Most partners look for exciting niches when building their first location. You want to promote high ticket items and make big financial profits. If gardening is mentioned as a possible niche, it can result in a raised eyebrow or two.

This is despite the fact that the horticultural industry in North America is currently valued at more than $ 70 billion a year.

People love gardening regardless of the growth of farms and urban agriculture. It's also worth noting that some of the most well-known hacking alumni in the horticultural industry have made serious money. How serious? 7 numbers a year.

52. Credit card

I remember the first time I saw big affiliate income. It's been about 15 years since a friend showed me what they'd done with offers from credit card partners.

When you know that a monthly income of $ 60,000 is entirely possible, your perspective changes.

Now times have changed. The credit card partner no longer offers as much as it used to. And there is more regulation in the industry.

But there is still incredible demand for credit cards - that's why the industry is worth $ 3.2 trillion in the US alone. Here are the programs we would encourage if we entered that niche.

53. Mortgage

It's easy to assume that no one is looking for a mortgage these days.

What about the mortgage crisis ten years ago and the world that is now completely crazy? However, keep in mind that assumptions are not a good idea when it comes to creating affiliate websites. This is because 89% of US mortgage applications are approved.

In short, the mortgage industry is booming, with thousands of new mortgages added every week. Some of the affiliate programs pay up to $ 200 per lead. So you do the math.

54. WordPress

Most of the websites you visit regularly are powered by WordPress, as WordPress has made web publishing accessible.

You don't need to know HTML or CSS or PHP to run a WordPress site. It also came up with the idea of blogging as a hobby or business.

Due to the enormous popularity of the platform, there is a demand for hosting, tools and other services. Believe it or not, it has created a sub-sector worth about $ 140 billion a year.

55. Web hosting

If you haven't lived under a rock, you know that web hosting affiliate programs can be insanely profitable.

For those of you who have lived in some kind of cave, read the information above. But is there still money in this niche? Remember, 547,000 new websites are created every day.

Each of these websites are hosted somewhere and they have likely signed up for their account through an affiliate link. And with average commission rates of $ 100 per sale, affiliates make a ton of money promoting web hosting offers.

Is it a competitive niche? Not if you are smart about how you handle your content marketing.

56. Fashion

An ideal niche is one where people are actively spending money, but are also recession-resistant.

These people - even during a major economic downturn - will continue to buy the products you are promoting. And strangely enough, fashion is one of those "perfect" niches. Because when everything else in their life has gone to hell, people still want to look and feel good. Even in times of war.

Another interesting fact is that online fashion is currently experiencing tremendous growth with sales growing at around 25% per year. You will also be amazed at how much commission some of these programs pay.

57. Software

I remember my first computer - a Sinclair ZX81 with 1 KB (yes, a kilobyte) of RAM. At this point you have entered "software" on the pages of a magazine.

The software industry is a completely different beast these days. New applications appear every day to help you with everything from task management to image editing. It has become an incredibly competitive industry to get involved in.

That's why, pretty much every software you can think of, has some sort of affiliate program. Some of them are happy to pay you up to $ 50 for referring a new customer. Software is probably one of the most overlooked niches in the affiliate marketing world.

58. Skincare

Skincare is one of those niches where the public spends much of its disposable income on products or services.

Because, as much as we don't like to admit it, humans are vain creatures.

We have been using beauty products for at least 7,000 years. And that's what we'll likely be doing for the next millennia.

But what's the skin care industry worth today? In North America alone, it's a whopping $ 180 billion, and that number is set to grow significantly over the next five years.

59. Binary options

Binary options are an important part of the global currency trading market. And while it's impossible to pinpoint any exact value, you can be pretty sure that this market is worth trillions of dollars.

The programs listed in this overview are a mix of exchanges, brokers, and training programs. Each of the brokers and exchanges are regulated so that your visitor's money is safe with them.

Basically, there is something here for almost every aspect of an audience interested in binary options trading. And earn some money with it.

60. SAAS

SaasA stands for Software As A Service, or software that you rent monthly but never own. So every web-based service you pay for is a SAAS product.

The great thing is that most of the big software companies do everything they can to get their products in the cloud instead of your local hard drive. That means there are tons of affiliate programs to promote, including many of the products and services that you already use.

This market is currently valued at around $ 600, but huge growth is expected in the years to come.

61. Loan repayment

A certain percentage of people will always get into financial trouble.

It doesn't matter if the economy goes up or down - some people are just "bad" with money. And all without the risk of an omnipresent recession or a downturn on the horizon.

So there will always be a demand for credit repair services and their affiliate programs. And since this is an ever-green niche, the website you're building today will likely still be pouring money into your bank account in ten years' time.

That cannot be said for many "popular" niches.

Bonus Affiliate Programs

This is a bit like the end credits scene in a Marvel movie.

So far, we have discussed specific niches and their programs. But we've also published content that focuses on two other key areas: deals that you pay a lot of money for, and those that you pay for more than once.

Recurring Affiliate Programs

My martial arts teacher once said this insightful phrase to me: "Why break a joint when you can break two?" You can also use this logic as an affiliate marketer: why not get paid multiple times for a single sale? This is exactly what recurring programs offer.

The downside to this is that most recurring programs only pay a few dollars a month. So if you have 4 repeat customers paying you $ 9 a month, you are not buying the Caribbean island you have always dreamed of. But 100 repeat customers paying you $ 900 a month is certainly good for your financial health.

Well-paid affiliate programs

It is very easy to find programs that promise to pay you (the affiliate) a lot of money. However, it is much more difficult to find those who have kept that promise.

CHAPTER FOUR

THE 8 AFFILIATE MARKETING SKILLS EVERY SUCCESSFUL AFFILIATE NEEDS

It takes a special kind of person to know about affiliate marketing.

We are not specialists. To be successful, we have to become experts in various fields. We almost all start alone and are forced to wear different hats.

As an affiliate marketer, you need to solve one problem at a time, manage your team, create ads, negotiate with people, and manage your money.

There is a term in the business world called "T-Shaped" skills. It means being an expert in one field while having a broad knowledge of several other disciplines.

Here are the 8 most important skills you should learn:

1. Problem solving and decision making

Affiliate marketing means you are constantly solving problems.

Have you experienced a massive loss of clicks from one day to the next? Has a competitor just entered your territory and outbid you? The hard part is that you run into problems and issues that no one else can help you with.

There is no manual to consult. The only people who can help you are your competitors, and you don't want to reveal your valuable campaign data to them.

Decision making is just as important. Most people rely on their gut instinct to make decisions.

When you have multiple niches to choose from, how do you decide which ones to pursue?

The good news is that you can learn how to become a better problem solver and decision maker. This is what I recommend to study psychology. I study cognitive prejudice intensively.

Use tools such as logical trees and decision matrices.

Learn strategies for making better decisions. Consult with experts, review all options, and make rational decisions instead of being impulsive.

2. Creativity and marketing

This is affiliate marketing, so it is necessary to be a good marketer in this business.

Creativity can help you find interesting angles for your campaigns.

While you can make money by copying other affiliates, my most successful campaigns are the ones I've innovated.

The first mover benefit in affiliate marketing is huge. To take advantage of this, you have to be creative.

In addition to angles, you also need to learn how to write compelling ads and a good copy of the landing page.

Our job is to sell and get people to work.

Your potential John is just browsing Facebook for fun. So you have to be very convincing if you want him to pull out his credit card and pay $ 50 for your product

How should you improve your marketing?

I would start by understanding the psychology behind buying from people. What are your motivations? Which words let you buy?

Study copywriting. Check out other marketers.

3. Technical ability

As an affiliate marketer, some basic technical knowledge is required.

You need to learn how to create landing pages, set up your tracker and deal with various issues you may encounter. This is the absolute minimum of technical knowledge you will need.

My friend is a brilliant programmer and uses his skills a lot. He showed me his setup on Skype a few months ago and it blew me away. He designed his own software that optimizes his offerings according to a formula. He had a dashboard made so that his employees only had access to parts of the campaign.

While you can outsource a lot of the technical chores, I recommend all affiliate marketers understand the basics of programming.

4. Human skills

Affiliate marketing isn't as people-centric as some other industries, but developing social and communication skills will help you with that.

I owe a large part of my success to the relationships I have built in this industry. I have some connected managers who are my eyes and ears for what's really hot.

I invented the brain and started joint ventures with others. I would never have made up some aspects of affiliate marketing if it hadn't been for them.

I also have people at traffic sources who give me inside information that no one else has.

Most affiliates are clumsy and have the social awareness of a potato. The industry attracts introverts, and it doesn't help to work alone all day.

Just treat others as you would like to be treated. Don't let your ego keep you from making real connections just because you get good grades.

5. Data analysis

Affiliate marketing is all about buying traffic. These clicks tell a story.

The conversions show you what types of people like your product. Does a certain ad convert better? Are you only profitable at certain times of the day? Does Android Traffic Convert Better?

With these tips you can optimize your campaign.

It's easy for you now that we have so many tools to help us. At that point I had to download the SUBIDs and create pivot tables / charts in Excel myself. Fortunately, these days you can use tools like Voluum.com that make analyzing your data easier.

Work to improve your ability to analyze the data so that you can take the appropriate action. Make decisions based on data, not emotions.

6. Money management

Managing your money is essential to affiliate marketing as your cash flow is the lifeblood of your campaigns.

Start by being realistic about how much you earn. A profit of $ 10,000 is one thing, but much less when you consider business expenses, taxes and future campaign failures.

Watch your bank accounts like a hawk. I know when each transfer should arrive each week and I will contact the advertiser if the transfer is late. Make sure to cancel any services you are not using ($ 99 per month will be added). If you've deposited money in traffic sources that you no longer use, ask them for a refund.

Live under your booth. I know you're tired of hearing this, but the reason it repeats all the time is because it's true. I've seen too many people quit the industry because they lived a lifestyle they couldn't afford.

Use your money to make more money.

7. Productivity

Obviously, I'm obsessed with productivity.

We all have the same 24 hours a day, but some people get a lot more of it than others

People always tell me that they admire my discipline. What they don't know is that I was the laziest student at Georgia Tech.

I wasn't born this way and it took a lot of work to develop my skills. I started lifting weights and meditating. I block my social media during my main working hours. I work in 50 minute sessions.

All of this is correct. I can work more in 4 hours than others in 10.

I know brilliant affiliate marketers who are only earning 15% of their potential. Why? Because they are not motivated or focused enough.

8. Leadership

Sooner or later you will find that you are the bottleneck and you have to build a team.

Most of the super partners I know lead teams of people. I have internal employees who manage campaigns. I have virtual assistants to help me, and I have other people who are critical to my success (maids, accountants, etc.).

It's not easy and it's a skill you need to develop. You need to delegate tasks that train, motivate, and address any issues.

Too many skills?

Does that seem like too many skills to learn?

The good news is that you don't have to be an expert in all areas to be successful. Some are less important than others; others can be outsourced.

I'm terrible in the tech department. I could have spent time improving my coding skills, but I'd rather hire other people to catch up with my weakness. In the meantime, I choose to hone my skills in other areas such as problem solving, data analysis and marketing.

Another way to deal with your weakness is to think about the skills of your employees. If you have three disorganized people, find someone who can calm the mess.

What I've noticed is that people who are opposites make the best partnerships in affiliate marketing. Maybe you have a guy who is the "face" and can communicate well. The other type may be more of a data analyst and problem solver. This type of team will work well because the members are complementary.

If you are a beginner, it is important not to be too confident just because you have pre-existing skills.

Is there any benefit in being a programmer? Absolutely. But just because you're a programmer doesn't mean you will make a lot of money. There are other very important skills that you need to develop to ensure your success.

Conclusion

The journey of a thousand miles begins with a single step.

Nobody is born knowing how to be an affiliate marketer. Are you missing some important skills that I mentioned? Then develop an action plan for improvement in these areas.

I had ZERO skills when I started affiliate marketing and I had to slowly develop them all over time.

CHAPTER FIVE

ULTIMATE DIGITAL MARKETING STRATEGY

I t's probably safe to assume that much of your current marketing strategy is digital. Consumers and businesses are almost always online and on the go - and you want to reach them and see how they behave and where they spend their time.

But when you start a business, it seems that this ever-changing digital landscape can quickly become an overwhelming landscape. With a number of other tasks to be performed, how can you also efficiently create, optimize and maintain a flexible digital marketing strategy?

I've created this chapter on marketing strategies that can help you improve your digital presence and grow better.

What is a Marketing Strategy?

It is important to understand how a marketing strategy differs from a digital marketing strategy before implementing either or both in your business.

A marketing strategy is a plan to achieve a specific marketing goal (or goals) in a targeted and achievable manner. It takes into account what your business is doing well in right now and what you're missing from the goal you've set so you're likely to achieve it.

But what's the difference between a marketing strategy and a marketing tactic - two marketing strategies vs. tactics

As mentioned above, a strategy is an attainable and targeted set of steps you can take to achieve a specific goal.

Marketing or not, each strategy has three parts: 1) a diagnosis of your challenge, 2) a guideline for dealing with the challenge, and 3) a series of targeted actions required to achieve the guideline.

Depending on the size of your business, your marketing strategy may include different moving parts, each with different goals. With this in mind, it can become daunting over time to work on your strategy. If you ever feel overwhelmed with your marketing strategy, read these three steps to focus on achieving your goals.

Marketing tactics or other tactics are the specific actions that you will choose during your strategy to achieve your end goal. In other words, a strategy is your goal - it's the feasible, focused plan to get you there. Tactics are concrete and definable steps within your strategy that will ensure that you achieve your goal.

Review the following list of basic marketing strategies commonly used by teams in various industries to better understand what they can mean.

Basic Marketing Strategies

- Publish a blog.
- Advertising on certain social media platforms (e.g. Facebook ads, Instagram ads).
- Offer free learning resources
- A Search engine optimizes your digital content.
- Create a giveaway and / or competition.
- Test different types of campaigns to see which ones are best for your target audience.
- Organize a webinar.
- Produce a podcast.
- Create an email campaign.

BONUS: What is a digital marketing strategy?

A digital marketing strategy is a plan that allows your business to achieve specific digital goals through carefully selected online marketing channels such as paid, earned, and proprietary media.

As with marketing strategies and marketing tactics, some other similar terms that are often mistakenly used interchangeably are digital marketing strategy and digital marketing campaign. How are they different?

What is a digital marketing campaign?

As mentioned earlier, a digital strategy is the set of actions you plan and take to achieve your overall digital marketing goal. Digital marketing campaigns, on the other hand, are the building blocks and actions within your strategy that lead you to a specific digital end goal.

For example, if the overall goal of your digital marketing strategy is to generate more leads through social media, you can run a digital marketing campaign on Twitter. You can share some of your company's top performing gated content on Twitter to drive more leads through the channel.

Next, let's look at the steps required to create a digital marketing strategy for your business.

How to Create a Digital Marketing Strategy

Create your buyer's personalities.

Identify your goals and the digital marketing tools you need.

Assess your existing digital channels and assets.

View and plan your own media campaigns.

Identify your goals and the digital marketing tools you need.

View and schedule your earned media campaigns.

1. Create your buyer's personalities

For any marketing strategy - digital or not - you need to know who you're marketing to. The best digital marketing strategies are based on detailed buyer personalities. Your first step is to make these.

Organize your audience segments and strengthen your marketing with templates to build the personalities of your buyers.

Buyer personalities represent your ideal customers and can be created through research and polling your company's target audience.

It's important to note that this information should be based on real-world data whenever possible, as assumptions about your target audience can cause your marketing strategy to go wrong.

To get a complete picture of yourself, your research pool should include a mix of customers, prospects, and people outside of your contact database who are aligned with your target audience.

But what kind of information do you need to gather for your own buyer personalities to teach your digital marketing strategy?

That depends on your business - it probably depends on whether you're B2B or B2C, or whether you're selling a high or low cost product.

Here are a few starting points you can fine-tune for your business.

Quantitative and Demographic Information:

- *Location*: Use web analytics tools to easily determine where your website traffic is coming from.
- *Age*: Depending on your company, this may or may not be relevant information. If it is, your best bet is to collect this data by identifying trends in your existing prospect and contact database.

- *Income*: It's best to keep confidential information, such as: Earning personal income, through personal research interviews, as people may not want to share these details through online forms.

- *Job Title*: This is something that can give you a rough idea of your existing customer base and is most relevant to B2B businesses.

- Qualitative and psychographic information:

- *Goals*: Depending on the challenge your product or service solves, you may already have a good idea of your buyer person's goals. Confirm your assumptions by speaking to real customers as well as internal sales and customer service reps.

- *Challenges*: Talk to customers, sales and service reps, and other customer-facing employees to understand the general challenges your audience is facing.

- *Hobbies / Interests*: Ask customers and those who match your target audience about their hobbies and interests. For example, if you are a fashion brand, it is helpful to know if large parts of your audience are also interested in fitness and wellness to inform them of future content and partnerships.

- *Priorities*: Talk to customers and viewers to find out what is most important to them about your business. For example, if you are a B2B software company, knowing that your audience values customer support above a competitive price is very valuable information.

By combining all of these details, you can create buyer personalities who are accurate and of great value to your business.

2. Identify your goals and the digital marketing tools you need

Your marketing goals should always be linked to the basic goals of your company.

For example, if your company's goal is to increase online sales by 20%, your marketing team's goal might be to generate 50% more leads through the website than last year to contribute to that success.

Use a high-level marketing plan template to outline your annual marketing strategy, identify top priorities, and more.

Whatever your overall digital marketing goal, you should be able to measure the success of your strategy along the way with the right digital marketing tools

For example, the reporting dashboard in HubSpot brings all your marketing and sales data together in one place, so you can quickly see what is and isn't working to improve your strategy for the future.

3. Assess your existing digital channels and assets

When reviewing your existing digital marketing channels and resources to determine what to include in your strategy, it's helpful to look at the bigger picture first. This will keep you from feeling overwhelmed or confused.

Collect what you have and categorize each vehicle or asset in a spreadsheet so that you have a clear view of your existing owned, earned and paid media.

Owned, earned and paid media management:

To do this effectively, use your owned, earned and paid media framework to categorize the digital "vehicles", assets, or channels already in use and decide what works well for your strategy.

Owned Media: This refers to the digital assets owned by your brand or company - be it your website, social media profiles, blog content or images. Private channels are where your company has full control.

This may also include external content that you own which is not hosted on your website (e.g, a blog that you post on Medium).

Earned Media: Earned Media refers to the level of exposure you get from word of mouth. Whether it's content you've shared on other websites (e.g Guest posts), PR work you've done, or the customer experience you've delivered. Merited Media is the recognition you will receive as a result of these efforts.

You can earn media by receiving press releases and positive reviews, and by sharing your content through their networks (e.g. social media channels).

Paid Media: Paid media refers to any vehicle or channel that you spend money on to attract the attention of your buyers' personality.

These include, for example, Google AdWords, paid social media posts, native advertising (e.g. sponsored posts on other websites) or other media through which you pay, in exchange for better visibility.

Let's look at an example to better understand what this framework entails.

Suppose you have your own content on a landing page on your website that was created to generate leads. They know that you want to include different parts of the framework instead of just working with owned, earned, or paid media.

To increase the number of leads the content generates, do your best to make sure it can be shared so your audience can spread it through their social media profiles. In turn, this will increase the traffic to your landing page. This is the media component earned.

To help your content succeed, post information about the content on your Facebook Page and pay to have more people in your audience see it.

This allows the three parts of the framework to work together - although this is not required for success. For example, if both your owned and earned media are already doing well, you might not need to invest in paid media. So, evaluate the best solution to achieve your goal, then incorporate the channels that are best for your business into your digital marketing strategy.

Now that you know what's already in use, it's time to start thinking about what to keep and what to cut.

4. Audit and plan your owned media campaigns

The core of digital marketing is owned by the media - and it almost always comes in the form of content. This is because almost any message your brand sends can be classified as content, be it a web page, about us, product descriptions, blog posts, e-books, infographics, podcasts or social media. Media Contributions.

Using content, you can convert your website visitors into leads and customers while enhancing your brand's online presence. And when that content is optimized for search engines (SEO), it can increase your search and organic traffic.

Regardless of the purpose of your digital marketing strategy, you want to include your own content. First, determine what content will help you achieve your goals.

If you want to generate 50% more leads from the website than last year, most likely your About page will not be included in your strategy unless this page has been a lead generation machine in the past.

Here's a quick process you can use to find out which of your own content you need to achieve your digital marketing strategy goals.

View your existing content

List your existing owned content and rank each item based on what previously worked best for your current goals.

For example, if your goal is lead generation, organize your content based on which areas generated the most leads in the past year (eg, a blog post, ebook, or website page).

This is about figuring out what works and what doesn't so you can prepare for success in planning future content.

Identify gaps in your existing content

Use the personalities of your buyers to identify any gaps in your content. For example, if you're a math teacher and you know through research that finding effective learning methods is a major challenge for your personas - you currently have no content to speak on that matter - make some.

If you look at your content rating, you will notice that ebooks hosted on a certain type of landing page convert very well (for example, better than webinars). In the case of this math tutoring company, you could make the decision to add an ebook to your content creation plans on how to make learning more effective.

Schedule content creation

Based on your results and the gaps you have identified, create a content creation plan that includes the content necessary to achieve your goals.

This contains:

- Title
- Format

- Target
- Advertising channels
- Why you are creating the content
- Content priority

This can be a simple spreadsheet and should also include budget information if you plan to outsource the creation of the content, or an estimate of the time if you are creating your own.

5. Monitor and plan your deserved media campaigns

By comparing your previously earned media with your current goals, you can get an idea of where to focus your time. See where your traffic and leads are coming from (if that's your goal), and rank each earned media source from most effective to least effective.

Chances are that a particular article you contributed to the industry press brought a lot of qualified traffic to your website and resulted in conversions. Or, you may find that LinkedIn is where most people share content, which increases traffic.

The idea is to use historical data to get a sense of what types of earned media will help you (and which will not) help you achieve your goals. However, if you want to experiment with something new, don't rule it out just because it has never been done before.

6. Monitor and plan your paid media campaigns

Much of this process involves the same process: you need to evaluate your existing paid media on each platform (e.g., Google

AdWords, Facebook, Twitter, etc.) to see what is likely to help you meet your current goals.

If you've spent a lot of money on AdWords and haven't seen the results you hoped for, it may be time to refine your approach or ignore it altogether and focus on another platform that seems to be producing better results.

Read this free guide to learn more about how to use AdWords for your digital marketing strategy

At the end of the process, you should have a clear idea of which paid media platforms you want to keep using and which (if any) you want to remove from your strategy.

7. Bring your digital marketing campaign together

You've done the planning and research and now you have a good idea of the elements that make up your digital marketing strategy.

To check this, you need to record the following:

- Clear profiles of your buyer's personality (s)
- One or more specific digital marketing objectives
- An inventory of your existing, earned and paid media
- A review of your existing owned, earned and paid media
- Your own plan for creating content or wish list

Now is the time to bring everything together in one coher-ent strategy document. Let's think about what digital strategy means: the set of actions you can take to achieve your goals through (digital) online marketing.

That said, your strategy paper should describe the set of actions you will take to achieve your goals based on your previous research.

(Pro tip: a table is an efficient format for this. For consistency, it may be easiest to map it using the previously used framework for your owned, earned and paid media.)

You'll also need to plan your long-term strategy - usually 6 to 12 months is a good place to start, depending on your company. That way, if you and your team take all action, there can be some overlap. For example:

In January, you start a blog that is updated once a week throughout the year.

In March, start a new e-book accompanied by paid ads.

Prepare for your biggest business month in July. At this point, what do you hope to have noticed that affects the content you are producing in support of this month?

In September, focus on earned media in the form of PR to generate additional traffic in advance.

With this approach, you create a structured timeline for your activity that you can use to communicate plans between colleagues.

Finally, here are some well-known examples of digital marketing campaigns and the strategies they use to inspire you.

Examples of Digital Marketing Campaigns

1. GoPro: Earned Media User-Made Video

GoPro is known for its unique point of view, all captured with the company's classic fisheye lens.

What you may not know is that so much of the video content you see on GoPro's YouTube channel was not created by GoPro, but by their loyal users.

By filling the YouTube channel with user-created video content, GoPro has encouraged the fan base to record their recordings and adventures and then post them online (thanks to the GoPro product for their recordings and experiences).

This ongoing digital marketing campaign encourages the use of videos to promote the GoPro product line and has created a community of loyal customers and fans.

2. Delta Air Lines: Twitter stories in the home media

Delta Air Lines is a prolific social media user, especially on Twitter. The brand uses the platform to approach potential passengers in a variety of ways that are both topical and emotionally stimulating.

During Breast Cancer Awareness Month, the company shared some personal stories of Delta employees through the company's Twitter profile.

This type of digital campaign drives loyalty, positive brand awareness, and gives potential and current customers an idea of what Delta is interested in and what it stands for.

3. Geico: Paid Media YouTube Preroll Ads

When you hear the word "Geico", many people automatically think, "You can save 15% or more on car insurance".

But even a company with such a catchy and successful slogan can risk annoying viewers (repetitive things can get old quickly) if a marketing campaign gets too boring.

That's why Geico has posted a series of pre-roll ads on YouTube that confirm the brevity of the ad. Preroll ads are a form of paid content on YouTube where you pay YouTube to show ads that take 15-20 seconds for videos to target the same audience as the advertiser.

While some companies try to get as much news as possible into this short slot, Geico took the opportunity to let their brand take their time.

This makes Geico's pre-roll commercials on YouTube fun and unique, and shows how secure the brand is.

4. Wayfair: Media-obsessed Instagram tags

Wayfair, an interior design and decoration retailer, has an innovative Instagram strategy: its Instagram photos are not just photos.

That's because Instagram allows businesses to create buy pages within the platform.

With Instagram Shopping, Wayfair published indoor photos on Instagram and provided the products in the photos with information and prices.

This is a digital marketing campaign that shows people exactly how much each item in the photos costs. It also instructs viewers to purchase the items in the photos without ever leaving the app. In return, Wayfair can increase conversions and revenue within Instagram.

5. Mastercard: Obsessed Media Travel Blog

Mastercard bases its brand on the stories and adventures that cardholders experience. But what use is a travel-based brand without an accompanying travel-based digital marketing campaign?

Priceless Cities, Mastercard's travel blog, is a tool that customers associate with the credit cards they use to pay for their trips.

This campaign allows the company to better customize its customers' investments and the places their customers travel to.

6. ETF Securities: Paid Media LinkedIn Sponsored Content

ETF Securities is a small asset management service for asset managers and investors in Europe.

The company found that its customers spend most of their time on LinkedIn interacting with sponsored, paid content on the platform.

By investing their time here, ETF Securities has increased interest in investing and helped their clients make smarter financial decisions. With this digital campaign, ETF Securities saw a 95% year-over-year growth in LinkedIn followers.

7. Red Bull: Lifestyle news from the media

Red Bull is known for sponsoring extreme sports, not just the energy drink they sell.

Rather than creating digital content around the energy drink, Red Bull manages to captivate its audience with articles and videos about the latest events in the extreme sports community.

In one of their digital marketing campaigns, Red Bull proved that what you sell isn't always the ideal focus for a content strategy. Rather, it can be much more valuable to tailor a campaign to the lifestyle your customers live with or want to be associated with.

Better growth with marketing strategies that strengthen your digital presence

Your strategy document is very individual to your business, which is why it is almost impossible for us to create a unified digital marketing strategy template.

Remember, the purpose of your strategy paper is to identify the actions you will take over time to achieve your goal. As long as this communicates, you master the basics of creating a digital strategy.

3 High-Impact Marketing Strategies You are Probably Overlooking

Everyone wants to be the first in his field, especially when it comes to marketing.

Reaching the top of search engine results and creating content that becomes viral is a marketer's dream — but it's often not that simple.

Creating performing and high-quality marketing campaigns means building content that fits with your company goals, brand voice, and target audience's interests.

It needs to be effective without breaking the budget or exceeding the problems which your team might be up against.

Remember, building a strong digital presence takes a lot of time and patience. Marketing campaigns will be effective once you've invested in properly defining your brand authority, messaging, and value proposition.

Fortunately, you can implement these three high-impact marketing strategies for your company to see maximum results. Here, we'll dive into the top three highly effective campaigns you should use for both quick successes, and great long-run results.

1. It's More Than Just LinkedIn: Account-Based Marketing

LinkedIn Ads are the leading tool for generating new leads in B2B in 2021, and a great start to any Account-Based Marketing campaign.

On LinkedIn you can target by location, job title, company, and more, that can help you reach the target people at the right time.

But you don't have to stop there. You need to build the trip beyond the ads. For instance, how and when will you nurture leads, who will nurture them, and where?

To maximize engagement with your Account-Based Marketing campaign, combine it with an inbound campaign. Build your infrastructure of additional content and emails to give value to your new leads and keep them engaged with your brand. Be sure to constantly refresh your content to maintain relevance and new interest in their minds.

Here's a five-step plan for building an effective ABM campaign with deep tactics:

Identify a campaign owner and make sure all team members shop across the company.

Create a LinkedIn Lead Generation campaign targeting the industry of your ideal company with compelling ads.

Create or update existing landing pages and content that speaks directly to the target audience. Customize the messages and design to draw attention and to bond with them.

Set up a workflow that incorporates and feeds the new leads with the above content, as well as dedicated landing pages, for advanced campaigns, set nurturing for each company or industry with custom messages and content for each.

Track leads and their engagement so you can connect with the right content at the right time.

2. Two are better than one: partnerships

An underestimated source of effective marketing is working with partners, give it importance. Finding someone to create content with is very effective and useful in terms of both cost and commitment.

Partners have a different perspective and can provide insights you may not have thought of. In addition, the back links are valuable from an SEO perspective. The resources you create with your partner can be shared with both your brand's networks. This will increase your presence and reach new target groups.

Simple ways to build these partnerships include posting a guest blog post, inviting a speaker to a webinar, or creating an info graph that showcases the expertise of both companies.

Make sure you choose your partners wisely. Your partner needs to share values, have a strong following, and add value to your target audience.

At the beginning of 2020, for example, our company planned to host a Hubspot User Group (HUG) on the Google Campus in Tel Aviv. After the pandemic and the resulting social distancing, all plans were lifted and companies had to adapt quickly. Suddenly, physical encounters were no longer an option.

To solve this, we decided to organize a virtual event in less than three weeks. Thanks to a dedicated workforce and strong partnerships, some of the industry's top marketing executives reached out to us to attend the event.

The involvement of these executives resulted in snowballs from their networks interested in attending the event. Although our HUGs are usually limited to 300 registrants for reasons of space, we were able to accept over 1,200 registrants for the virtual event.

3. Actions speak louder than words: customer evangelism

Customer evangelism is arguably one of the most powerful tools for generating potential leads. You can create great campaigns, but nothing compares to a shared recommendation from a happy customer

The incoming flywheel consists of three parts; Attract, involve and delight. If you don't make your customers happy, your fly-wheel won't be able to reach top speed.

A customer evangelization program is not a linear campaign. You have to surprise your customers at all points of contact. When the opportunity arises, they will be happy to recommend you to their network.

In addition to impeccable service and great results, consider other creative ways to connect with customers and build rela-tionships. This can be anything from social media shout outs for victories to sending New Years greetings to show that you are thinking about them. Ultimately, a little generosity can go a long way.

Recently, one of our clients was on LinkedIn when he came across a message from a connection who had never heard of us. Our client was very happy with our services and suggested that he should check us out. A day later, he was talking to a salesperson who became a new customer.

You are already in constant contact with your customers and they have an infinite amount of potential to acquire new customers - don't neglect the opportunity.

These strategies are only the first step in building an effective marketing strategy. They need to be combined with a full strategic plan tailored to your entire business, from marketing and sales to customer success and much more.

Each campaign is just one piece of a larger marketing puzzle that has to cover all phases of the marketing strategy. No campaign can live alone.

Additionally, it's important to monitor old campaigns to earn insights and be sure that you optimize each future campaign to improv results.

CHAPTER SIX

FREE VS PAID TRAFFIC

With traffic you bring potential customers to your landing page. Let me explain free and paid traffic with an analogy. Say you have a restaurant and you want more customers. How do you bring more customers to the restaurant? Marketing.

Now there are two ways of marketing to get people to the restaurant. Free and paid.

Free methods:

- Leave someone outside with a sign.
- Advertise a special on your Facebook page.
- Encourage customers to leave a review on Yelp for good reviews and recommendations.

Paid Methods:

- Buy an ad on TV.
- Rent a billboard to promote your offers.
- Pay a food blogger to rate your restaurant.

Do you see the difference between the two?

Free takes a lot of work. It's technically not free either, but it feels free because you aren't paying directly for ad space, billboards, or anything else.

Paid methods cost real money, but are much less repetitive. I hope this analogy helps you understand.

As a partner, we create landing pages to sell the offers we advertise. Your job is to attract potential customers to the landing pages. There are two main types of traffic: paid and free.

Free Traffic

There are a lot of different ways to get "free" traffic, but I want to discuss the main ways that partners work.

Content Marketing

You attract people by creating great content. Examples are blog articles, Facebook pages and YouTube videos.

You will become an expert in your niche, build a large following, and then you can make money by recommending different products and services.

For example; fitness people on YouTube. They build an audience by creating training videos and sharing great information. From there, people rely on their recommendations. You can advertise a supplement or exercise plan, people buy it, and the fitness guy gets a commission from everyone who buys it.

Search engine optimization aka "SEO"

SEO traffic refers to the organic results (also called natural results) on search engines. SEO stands for search engine optimization and refers to the process of optimizing your website so that it ranks higher in search engines.

There are quite a few tactics people use to rank their sites higher in the search results. You cannot pay Google to be number 1 in search results. You have to earn it.

I am about to explain how to get to number 1. But first ... did you know that when you search in a search engine you are not looking on the internet?

They are just looking for their "index". This means that you are only searching the website database of this search engine. Of course, Google has the largest index, which is why all other search engines just copy them.

SEO is an attractive resource because it is "free".

What could be better when BestBuy.com is # 1 in the "Big Screen TV" category? For this keyword alone, you get millions of visitors every month and you don't pay a cent for it.

Google has a complicated search algorithm that takes hundreds of variables into account to determine which website to rank for which keywords.

For example, a big variable in getting rankings is getting links. Google determines that your website is an important website when other popular similar websites link to it. So your website will rank higher than others with links of more or less high quality.

Knowing this, SEO folks try to get links in different ways, including money of course. (Google frowns and actively monitors paid links).

And that's just one of the variables SEO should consider (although it is arguably the most important variable). Trying to optimize this algorithm takes time, resources, and money.

Even after perfect optimization, it can take months to years to finally get a position for your target keyword.

Plus, Google is constantly updating its algorithm, so a single update could ruin ALL of your efforts.

If you've ever heard SEO people talk about penguin or panda then you know the dangers of relying 100% on SEO traffic as your primary source.

However, if you can solve the SEO conundrum and get placed on the first page for your keyword, congratulations. You get tons of free, targeted traffic.

Paid Traffic

There are advertisements all over the internet. You can purchase the advertising space to advertise your partner offer. You pay money every time someone clicks on your ad.

The 3 main payment methods:

- Cost per click (CPC) - you only pay when someone clicks on the ad. Example: you offer a CPC of $ 0.25. You pay a maximum of € 0.25 per click
- Cost per Million (CPM) - You pay for every 1000 views. Example: € 2 CPM. If your ad appears 10,000 times, you pay $ 20.
- Flat rate - you pay a flat fee regardless of the number of clicks / views. Example: I buy Ad Unit B for $ 500 for a week.

I know this sounds scary, but with paid traffic you have full control over everything.

You can set the budget. If you can only afford $ 10 a day, only $ 10 will be spent.

You can set the bids.

You can stop the campaign at any time. For example, if you want to spend $ 100 on a campaign BUT after you've lost $50 you're not so sure, you can pause it.

Why I'd rather get paid than free traffic

You probably think ... free traffic sounds a lot better! I thought the same when I started. Folks, nothing is really free.

If you use YouTube, it will take a long time to build your followers. I'm talking about years.

If you are going the SEO route, good luck. No, it's not free. You have to spend money on software and link building.

Yes, there are exceptions to the rule, but it usually takes a long, long time for "free" to pay off, if at all. You need to create content, grow your website, connect with people and networks, and a lot more.

That's why I prefer paid traffic:

Immediate results. You can start a campaign today and see if it's profitable in hours. Content Marketing? It can take years to build followers through blogging or YouTube. SEO? It can take up to 6 months before you see the fruits of your labor.

You are not dependent on a company. I had a friend who was focused on SEO for years. He woke up one day and all of his websites were destroyed by the latest Google update (Panda). He couldn't adapt. What should I do if my top 3 traffic sources stop working? I still have 100+ that I can use. That makes it easier for me to sleep at night.

You can make more money a lot faster with paid traffic. The top people in affiliate marketing can make 5 numbers in a day (even 6 numbers). Let's just say I've seen a lot of people switch from SEO to paid traffic and rarely see it the other way around. In my first year, I did a lot more than I ever thought possible.

There are hundreds and hundreds of different traffic sources that you can buy. I know it can be overwhelming, but that's a good thing.

One of the biggest problems in business is what I call "risk concentration". If your primary traffic source isn't working for you, you have other options.

What is the difference between the traffic sources?

1) The type of audience: what type of audience does ESPN have? Probably men who like sports. Do you think promoting women's shoes would be effective? No. Understand what kind of audience your traffic source is.

   Tip: You can ask your traffic source for a report on which countries have the highest volume. Sometimes they can even give you more detailed information such as age, gender and other demographic information.

   If you're into Singapore advertising a lot, wouldn't it make sense to work only with high traffic sources in Singapore?

2) The Targeting Options: Targeting is your ability to promote your ads to a selected segment of the target audience. The more targeting options the traffic source has, the better. Some examples of targeting options:

   - Age
   - Sex
   - The state they are in
   - Your favorite TV shows
   - The time of day your ad will appear

- Which device the person is using (mobile or desktop, iPhone vs. Android)
- The website they are visiting (also known as a placement or SiteID)

Targeting can help you get into the most profitable segments. Imagine you have a pet store. You spend $ 100 on 1,000 flyers. You want to place the flyers in the places where your audience is likely to be.

Placing them in grocery stores and Walmart CAN work, but they can be used more effectively. You can put them at places where people take their pets, e.g dog parks, and vets.

That's a big part of campaigning: you need to figure out who wants your offers, and then AIM at them.

Therefore, Google and Facebook are considered the main traffic sources. This is not only due to the amount of VOLUME they have, but also their AIM.

1) The cost: Each traffic source also has different payment options (different bidding models). A website can be too expensive because of the competition. Another could be a "hidden gem" and have many websites that get a lot of conversions.
2) Rules and Regulations: This is huge. Some traffic sources are stricter than others. This means that you limit yourself to what you can promote.

3) The available traffic volume: not every traffic source can generate 5 songs per day. I always tell people to make it big.

   Tip: If you're a newbie, don't worry if you don't hit the big grades. Big payouts will come later. Concentrate on making your first $ 100 a day.

4) The Competition: There are some traffic sources that are amazing and not too competitive. If there is a lot of supply and not many buyers, it can be undervalued.

5) The quality of the traffic source: "The leads are weak? No, you are weak! "

I'll tell you in a minute, some traffic sources are worthless. Maybe there is a lot of FRAUD traffic.

- You think the click you paid $ 0.50 for was a real converting person, but it was actually an editor's bot.
- You think the click was an iPhone user in Singapore. In fact, it was an Android user from Malaysia. Major traffic sources have the resources / people to reinvest in better technology so this doesn't happen that often.

The different types of paid traffic sources

There are hundreds of traffic sources available online and offline. The easiest way to understand the difference is to split them into different CATEGORIES.

Social Traffic: Social traffic sources relate to targeting users based on demographics, interests, or similar targeting options.

Social ad platforms qualify users based on options that advertisers target, such as: age, interest, geographic location, etc. If the user meets the advertiser's requirements, the ad will serve.

Social traffic allows creative advertisers to tailor ads to a specific user base. Social Traffic Sources:

- Facebook
- Lots of fish
- Pinterest

While there are tons of social networks to buy traffic from, let's focus on the biggest one: Facebook.

With a huge selection of targeting options and an almost unlimited range of traffic, Facebook is one of the most lucrative sources of affiliate traffic. Main test variables on Facebook:

- Age groups
- Interest keywords
- Bidding type

Search Traffic: Search traffic simply describes the traffic that comes from search engines.

To keep it simple, we're going to talk about Google, the largest search engine (and traffic source) in the world. Since Google is the largest search engine in the world, it is the most visited website in the world.

Google is a powerful and compelling source of traffic because it enables keyword targeting (the queries that are entered into the search box). You can show ads that are specific to users.

For example, if you type 'big screen TV' in Google, you will immediately see search results and search ads relevant to that query.

Note that two types of results are displayed:

1. Organic results
2. Results paid

Google's paid search platform is called AdWords. Advertisers can pay to be featured at the top for targeted keywords. Your cost per click is determined by the keyword you are bidding on and the relevance of your ad and website to that keyword.

Google's advertising platform is easy to use and has a wide variety of tools and settings that will allow you to create the most relevant, powerful, and affordable campaign in minutes.

Mobile Traffic: When branches refer to mobile as a traffic source, it means advertising on mobile phones. Mobile is the fastest growing source of traffic. What I like about mobile devices is that we can advertise in countries that we couldn't before.

5 years ago I couldn't imagine advertising in Indonesia, Iran and Colombia These countries now love cell phones and we can

generate income from them. Note that many traffic sources like Facebook and Google have desktop and mobile traffic.

Tip: Always set up separate campaigns for desktop and mobile. You don't want to confuse traffic because it performs differently.

The most popular forms of advertising in mobile communications are: advertisement / banner, pop-ups, and announcements

The biggest challenge with mobile devices is the optimization process. Improving a campaign is difficult enough. Now you need to add: carriers, operating systems, handsets, and more.

It can be difficult for many affiliates to see things like your website or ad correctly on all phones, or how quickly they load in order to optimize them.

However, the potential for mobile devices is enormous and the range extends across the whole world. Mobility as a source of traffic enables advertising in untapped markets around the world and enables cost-effective advertising with high ROIs. (In many countries, access to a mobile phone is much easier than a computer).

With its growing popularity, there are numerous traffic sources that specialize only in mobile traffic. There are even traffic sources that only specialize in certain types of mobile ads, such as "Mobile Pops" or "Mobile Display".

Native Ads: You saw this 'featured content' or 'sponsored stories' below or on the articles and news sites page.

Native ads provide a natural, native mix with articles. The public has generally gone blind to banner advertising. Native is a way for us to 'sneak' advertisements to people. Native advertising has been around for a long time, but its popularity has skyrocketed in the past two years.

The key to being native is getting cheap CPCs and competing for available traffic stock (site placements). Many local partners build relationships and ensure profitable placements.

Popular native traffic sources are: MGID, Taboola, Outbrain and Content.ad.

Be warned however, that native traffic sources are getting tougher (though not as strict as Facebook and Google) when it comes to advertising methods and offer types.

Adult Traffic: This means promoting offers on adult porn sites. It is estimated that 30% of all internet traffic is adult, so I wouldn't turn it down just yet. A big advantage of adult advertising is that the offers you are promoting are not that strict.

Main Key: Consider this a traffic source with a strongly male population. Everyone assumes that you can only advertise dating offers.

But do you think ... What else would a man care about?

The main sources of traffic for adults are TraffcJunky and Exoclick.

Adult traffic is attractive to partners because it offers HUGE traffic and a lot of freedom to advertise promotions.

Drawbacks include that the extreme competitive environment has caused the top positions on sites to be overcrowded with the same offerings, many key players making it difficult for newbies to enter the market, and difficult to send high quality leads to some offers.

PPV traffic: PPV (pay-per-view), also known as cost-per-view (CPV), is toolbar traffic.

PPV transport networks install toolbars on people's computers (with their permission) so that the network announces pop-ups on their computers. (Users are encouraged to install these toolbars so they can play games, win prizes, get free wallpapers, access the weather forecast, or other news.)

PPV mainly works with URL and keyword targeting. Advertisers can bid on URL Targets and / or Keyword Targets.

Here is an example of URL targeting: John visits www.geico.com. If the advertiser bids on "www.geico.com" when visiting www.geico.com, they will trigger a popup (usually an 800 x 600 ad) from the traffic source. The popup could be an ad promoting a competitor's auto insurance.

The PPV network receives all advertising revenue. An example of keyword targeting is: John goes to Google.com and types in "geico". If the advertiser bids on the keyword "Geico", John will see a popup.

Keyword targeting in PPV means that your ad will show when people enter the keyword in the search bar.

Interestingly, Geico does not receive any ad revenue, only the PPV network. This means you can advertise on sites like ESPN. com for only a fraction of that cost (usually very expensive).

The two most popular PPV networks are:

1. Drive media
2 50onRed

There is not much difference between the two. The minimum deposit for advertisers on both networks is $ 1000.

The benefits of PPV include:

- Landing pages are generally very simple with PPV.
- The advertising policies for PPV networks are much looser than most other traffic sources (which means you can be very aggressive in promoting a variety of offers).
- Targeting is cheaper than traditional traffic sources. (You can bid on URL destinations for a fraction of a cent).

The drawbacks are:

- There are not many sources of PPV traffic.
- These traffic sources require a high minimum deposit (1000 USD).
- The margins have become very small due to competition and saturation
- Traffic quality is mostly dead.

The central theses:

- There are huge differences between traffic sources, including costs, allowed costs, targeting options and population type.
- It is easier to understand traffic sources by dividing them into different categories.

CHAPTER SEVEN

TOP 3 FREE AFFILIATE MARKETING CHANNELS IN 2021

This chapter discusses the top three ways to build an affiliate marketing business based on traffic sources in 2021. This chapter can solve your "money problem" if you are planning to start a cheap business with no bottlenecks or earning term expectations.

As we shall see, creating a good digital channel is a real asset to your affiliate marketing business. You can combine this information with a paid traffic source to get the most from your business.

Let's get started, I'll show you what we'll cover in this chapter:

- How to Create Your Own Affiliate Blog
- Affiliate Marketing With YouTube: A Step-by-Step Guide
- The Definitive Guide to Affiliate Marketing on Instagram

How to Create Your Own Affiliate Blog

Are you ready to learn how to create your profitable affiliate blog?

Blogs that make money from affiliate sales are another common business model. They take a lot more work than some other online business models, but the rewards can be worth it considering how much bloggers make, as you'll read below.

Here's what you will learn:

- How to create your own blog that is profitable
- Pros and Cons of Affiliate Blogs - It's Not All Sunshine!
- How this business model delivers value and, in turn, brings you income.
- How to create your own affiliate blog in a few easy steps.
- How to Create Your Own Profitable Affiliate Blog

So we all know what a blog is. You've read one.

You can read here how to make an epic blog.

Blogs that make money through affiliate marketing do so by promoting products on their posts and / or through their email list.

Some choose not to promote the blog at all and only use it for email, while others choose not to email any promotions to subscribers and leave them on the blog. Both models have their advantages.

Typically, those bloggers who see real success with this model are honest and forthright about the fact that they receive commissions and deliver incredible value in every post.

They don't write fake reviews of products or say 'XYZ' is just great to promote. The most successful affiliate blogs are open, honest, and offer incredible value-packed content.

They show in action what they are promoting, write in-depth reviews, create case studies, provide actionable content for their visitors to see results from, and in turn, their visitors reward them by clicking on their links and buying.

So they are essentially behind what they are promoting and have mostly used the products themselves.

Their great content and all-important value makes their visitors start to trust and develop a relationship with them, and you are far more likely to buy from someone like them than from a random internet stranger.

Aside from content promoting something, most of your content is probably pure value that your visitor can use that doesn't promote anything.

Advantages and disadvantages:

Pros:

A Great way to build trust and reputation. This is the easiest way to advertise partner products.

Easily create an email list that you can use to develop your business by driving traffic back and promoting your website.

Earning affiliate commissions with relative ease through actionable content, case studies, and reviews.

Blogs are easy to direct - you get Google traffic, referrals from other bloggers, forum mentions, social media sharing, and so on, provided your content is good.

Cons:

Take the time to build your reputation as a trusted marketer with quality content.

80% of your content is unlikely to be promoting anything, so you've put a lot of work into writing and creating new posts that won't monetize right away - it will improve your credibility, traffic, and email list.

Not a quick way to make money in most cases, as you have to build your content and traffic before you can get any significant results.

How these websites deliver value:

By creating some of the best content in the niche on the topics your audience wants to know about. By solving their problems and providing them with actionable content that they can use to improve themselves or their situation. Never distribute content that is half-hearted or just intended to promote a product. Only promote products that you really believe in.

Solve your audience's problems, whether you get commission or not, and they'll buy whatever you recommend.

Examples of successful affiliate blogs

Matthew Woodward at matthewwoodward.co.uk:

He earns over $ 14,000 per month from affiliate sales alone. Matt's blog is an incredible example of an "affiliate blog" running properly. High quality content, detailed tutorials, articles, video instructions, honesty, openness, trust - that's exactly how it should be done.

In less than 2 years he has built a solid reputation as a blogger that you can trust and in return people are happy to click on his affiliate links.

Lindsay at PinchofYum.com:

She earns about $ 20,000 a month in affiliate sales. I am presenting this cooking blog so that we don't just focus on internet marketing blogs. And to show that it is possible to make money with affiliate marketing without giving affiliate marketing advice.

Lindsay makes money with different kinds of programs, from WordPress themes to cookbooks to MailChimp, online yoga classes and much more.

Pat Flynn at SmartPassiveIncome.com:

Income of $ 67,000 + p / m from affiliate sales on his blog alone, excluding product sales and revenue from other websites.

Pat has been blogging at SPI since 2008 and was one of the first marketers to honestly and openly report his income through monthly earnings reports.

He is not afraid to be in front of the camera, he is not afraid to share his life, he is open, he is honest, he puts himself out and ALWAYS delivers more than necessary.

He never advertises anything unless he has used it himself, and he not only advertises for you but shows you how YOU can make the most of it. All of this leads to a profitable affiliate company for him.

How you can create your own profitable affiliate blog

Pick your niche, make sure there is high demand and that there are many related products for sale with an easily accessible audience. Your main focus is on your content. Make it epic. Do it better than almost any other content out there.

Take a look at the type of content that is already getting a lot of links and shares and do something bigger and better. This is what is called the "skyscraper technique".

Or search for general questions on specific topics in forums on your topic and turn them into the "ultimate guide".

Network like crazy with others in your niche. Link them, share their content, comment on their blogs, email them, do something cool for them for free.

If it's done right, they will return the favor IF it's worth sharing your content and linking to the back. Be where your target audience is online.

Guest posts on popular blogs get active in the busy forums, get involved in social media pages and groups to attract more visitors.

Show yourself to be someone knowledgeable, helpful, friendly, and approachable and bring your content to them.

Make yourself the main goal of your blog to build your email list as it will speed up your websites success and bring traffic back to your new blog posts.

It will also help you build your relationship with your audience faster and increase your income through email promos (if you choose to).

Earn from the start. Don't make the mistake of waiting for a "good time" or until you have an "X" number of subscribers because that's a waste of time.

Your first visitor to your blog doesn't know they are the first to visit, and if you add value to them there is no reason why # 1 visitor isn't buying something that you recommend.

A blog is nothing without great content BUT you also have to work hard to promote this content or no one will ever see it.

What you need to get started

A noticeable and memorable domain.

An autoresponder from day one that can help you build, sky-rocket, and monetize your email list.

Get content ideas by finding popular content in your niche using the "skyscraper technique" or by finding FAQs in your niche and creating the most epic content you can.

Network and build relationships with others in the niche through contact, exchange, linking and presentation.

Honesty, openness and reliability of your product recommendations.

Affiliate Blog Summary

Affiliate marketing through a blog is usually not a short-term way to make money, although it is long-run and sustainable.

It allows you to build a relationship and trust with your audience and be considered an authority in your niche, which in the case of Pat Flynn has resulted in an income of $ 60,000 per month.

With your great content, you can build your email list and pro-mote affiliate products.

Because of the increased trust, honesty and openness, and the value you provide, people are happy to buy based on your recommendations.

Affiliate marketing blogging works in numerous niches, from internet marketing to cooking / recipes, as we saw in the examples above.

Making the affiliate blogging model a great way to make money from it.

Affiliate Marketing With YouTube in 2021: A step-by-step Guide

What is YouTube affiliate marketing?

YouTube affiliate marketing is the process of making money by creating videos that encourage viewers to purchase recommended products through affiliate links posted in the videos themselves (via annotations) or in the video descriptions.

There are many opportunities to promote products and services and earn commissions for affiliates in 2021. Affiliate marketing itself is an issue about the size of the Pacific.

Wikipedia defines that affiliate marketing is "a type of performance-oriented marketing in which a company rewards one or more affiliate companies for each visitor or customer that is generated by the affiliate's own marketing efforts".

The 5 Step Guide to Becoming a YouTube Affiliate Marketer

I'll tell you honestly, if you follow these 5 steps to a "T" you will benefit from affiliate commissions over time.

The free and easiest way to get started as a YouTube partner is by rating products. It's as simple as that.

Most of us already use many products that others would like to receive honest feedback about, such as: Advantages and disadvantages as well as purchase recommendations.

Key Takeaway: After all, if you create a high quality YouTube channel that constantly displays engaging, great content that people want to see, you will end up getting more and more exposure to your videos.

More eyeballs mean more sales and commissions. It really is a numbers game.

Here are the 5 steps to starting your own YouTube affiliate program in 2021:

Step 1: Pick a niche and audience

For this step, you need to choose something that you are very passionate about and enjoy doing. You know what I mean?

If you are passionate you will create much more stylish videos.

Those who watch your videos will see your true passion and will likely want to see more of your YouTube channel. So choose what you are obsessed with e.g. If you are a bookworm, read books.

If you are a health freak who leads a healthy organic lifestyle, you should embark on your journey to try different brands and products, share their pros and cons, and recommend the ones you like.

Once you've made a list of niches, it's time to start thinking about who is watching your YouTube videos (your audience).

Step 2: Choose an affiliate program

There are many affiliate programs, but by far the simplest program is the Amazon Associate Program (note, however, that they recently cut their affiliate commissions in half).

Check out all of the products on Amazon and then recommend your favorites. If someone watches your video, then clicks on your affiliate links and makes a purchase, you will receive a commission. At this point you might ask, "But where can I find affiliate offers?"

Step 3: Set up your YouTube channel

Setting up a YouTube channel is extremely easy. Almost everyone already has a Gmail account. If you don't, just create a Gmail account and use it to sign in to YouTube.

There are tons of step-by-step videos out there to show you how to do this. In this guide, I'm going to focus on the things that actually get things moving.

Things that separate your channel and video content from the rest and help you get more views.

Part A: Creating a Professional YouTube Channel Layout

Pay special attention to the USP (Unique Selling Proposition) used in the YouTube cover photo. It gives you its website and its USP: "Marketing | Mindset | Motivation".

The USP for this niche should be something like "I read them all so you can just read what you like". You know what I mean.

Next, the profile picture should be a high quality photo of you. Headshots are the best.

Trailer Video: This is the main video on your YouTube profile that will automatically play when someone visits your channel.

This video should be relatively short depending on your niche. I recommend 2-3 minutes tops. It has to be an extension of your USP.

Organize videos by topic: If you are going to continue creating content, it is very important to organize your videos by topic.

This helps people navigate their desired topic. You stay on your channel longer. The longer people stay, the more likely they are to take action and earn you income.

Part B: Consistent Content Creation

Aside from the fact that practice makes you permanent and creating more and more content makes you a better content creator, there is another very practical reason to do it.

The YouTube algorithm favors channels that publish content consistently. As a professional content creator, you separate yourself from the potential users who don't regularly publish videos.

Part C: Write Enticing Titles

If your title doesn't engage, nothing else matters.

You can have the best, most engaging video content, but no one will see it if your title doesn't demonstrate it. Your video title only has one job. This allows the user to click and view your video.

Your video title works with your thumbnail to control opening and viewing of the video. We will discuss the thumbnails next.

There are many ways to write great titles. One possibility is to use incomplete titles. Here's an example: "This dangerous kitchen blender has my ..."

Part D: Attention to grabbing thumbnails

Thumbnails are still images for the video you see before playing. The combination of thumbnail and title can increase or decrease the success of your channels. So you have to do this right.

By default, your thumbnail is any photo from your video.

All professional content creators on YouTube design their own custom thumbnail images and then upload them to the specific video.

They do this because a thumbnail with markers like arrows, circles and authority logos increases the click-through rate of your videos.

Part E: Professional Descriptions

There is a formula in your video descriptions. You can get creative, but this layout works great.

The first thing you want to do is put one or more links that you want people to visit "above the fold".

These links can be your social media profiles, links to your website, affiliate links, and so on.

Your video description is a great place to find keywords that you want to rank for as well.

Part F: Spectators at S.C.L.(Subscribe, Comment and Like)

You will find it difficult to watch a professional YouTube video and not see instructions from the host on how to subscribe, comment and like.

You have to do this for a good reason. Your subscribers will be notified when you post new content. Like and comment on your video will help you with the search engine. Make sure you do this at least once per video. Most people do it until the end of the video which it's fine too, depending on your niche.

Part G: Carefully Placed Tags

Before you publish your video, it's a good idea to add tags. This is another way to help people find your videos organic. Most people post 2 or 3 broad categories here with a lot of attention.

Don't be one of them. Think a little more and mix broader keywords with longer ending versions of keywords to really improve your search engine results. Example: "earn money quickly online in 2021", "earn money quickly with ClickBank"

Part H: Subtitles

Many people omit these, but you should definitely do them. You get additional SEO juice and can position yourself better in the search engines.

It's also now easier than ever. There is an automatic subtitle feature that you can turn on when you upload a video. While this feature works fine, I recommend going through it manually, checking for errors, and making any necessary changes.

Part I: Tips for Making a Winning Video

ATTENTION:

You need to grab the viewer's attention for the first 3 to 5 seconds and involve them in the video content.

Start the content with a question. Open loops fascinate people and their minds must continue until they close the circle. Example: difficulty losing weight?

Bridge model - Talk about the situation you want (where you want to be). Then discuss where you are now. Finally, talk about a bridge to take you from your current situation to the desired situation.

REMARKS:

Annotations are also known as text overlays.

Annotations allow you to place text and / or website links over your video.

Annotations are a great way to increase engagement and click through rate.

Be careful not to go overboard however, as it can have the opposite effect and make viewers close your video.

CALL FOR ACTIONS

Every successful marketing campaign uses call-to-action. It doesn't matter whether the medium is TV, radio or social media. So YouTube is no exception. A "call to action" simply tells the viewer what to do next.

It's usually the step to making money. When marketing a book use the following as a call to action: "Click the link below for your copy."

The key to an effective call to action is to keep it short and sweet. Don't confuse the viewer with too many instructions. A confused mind says no or hesitates.

Step 4: Adding Your Affiliate Links

The most common place to add your affiliate link is on the description and above the crease. You can also add your affiliate links in notes. Point out the links during your video or at the end so the viewer can search for them there.

Step 5: Collect / Flush and Repeat Commissions

Collect your commissions and keep optimizing.

You can add advanced parts as well as your own website. If you have your own website, you can increase your affiliate commissions by building an email list of your YouTube subscribers.

Lots of people say email marketing is dead, but they couldn't be more wrong. When people know, like, and trust you, they will rave about your content and act on your recommendations.

The Definitive Guide to Instagram Affiliate Marketing

Among other things, influencers from all industries try to monetize their influence on social media by doing affiliate marketing on Instagram. With Instagram becoming so popular around the world and with an active and engaged audience, Instagram's affiliate marketing is one of the primary ways influencers can monetize their social media followers - one of nine ways I wrote in my article, "How To Earn Money On Instagram".

For influencers using Instagram as an affiliate marketer, the goal is to drive as much traffic as possible to their marketing partners' websites through their tracked links. Because Instagram has a higher engagement than Tumblr, Twitter and Snapchat - or any other social network - Instagram's affiliate marketing offers a variety of options once you join, whether as a brand that wants to promote products or as a an affiliate. . If everyone is promoting on Instagram, you should too!

This post looks at Instagram's affiliate marketing from both an influencer and brand perspective. Since this is going to be one of my longer sections, here's a quick bullet point summary so you know what to expect:

- How Instagram Affiliate Marketing Words - The Basics
- How can you promote links on Instagram if you cannot create links on Instagram?
- The benefits of Instagram Affiliate Marketing for brands
- What types of Instagram users will be successful in Instagram affiliate marketing?
- Popular affiliate marketing marketplaces
- Understand the disclosure laws of the FTC
- Transition from Instagram user to affiliate marketing on Instagram

Even if you are not interested in affiliate marketing through Instagram, this section should give you some tips on how to influence Instagram more!

So, how does Instagram affiliate marketing work?

It does this by building partnerships between a user who is the affiliate marketer and through some sort of introduction or promotion for a company's products or services on the marketer's website, social media, or wherever. The affiliate marketer displays the product or service in their posts and earns a commission for every sale that can be attributed to their post, e.g. via a URL link that is provided with a unique affiliate code. When these affiliate promotions are done on Instagram, we call it Instagram affiliate marketing, but affiliate marketing is clearly not limited to Instagram as a platform!

The brand that is advertised wins the interest of the customer, and the influencer profile that acts as an affiliate is used to attract its users to the advertised product. The influencer earns a share of the sale of the advertised product. Therefore, it is mutually beneficial for the brand and the influencers to work together. This is why affiliate marketing is influencer marketing's new best friend!

How can affiliates promote links on Instagram if they can't link on Instagram?

I'll cover some more specific advice for affiliate marketers later in this section, but one of the direct questions you are likely to have is related to blogs; Twitter, Facebook, LinkedIn, etc. Instagram doesn't allow you to post a link every time

you post a photo. How can affiliate marketers on Instagram get people to enter a link with their affiliate code in their browser and buy a product? There are actually a few options once you get creative and think outside the box:

Affiliate Link in Your Bio (Permanent): The obvious link is to use the link in your bio to direct people to the site. This works well when you're promoting the same brand, product, or link over and over again. Then you tell people to click the link in your bio. Ideal if you are a brand ambassador and exclusive partner of a brand.

Affiliate link in your bio (semi-permanent):

If you want to promote a different product with each post, you can still use the link in your bio, but you will need to update it every time you publish a new post. You can still tell people to click on the link in your bio. However, if someone discovers an older post promoting a different product, they land on a different landing page. So this is not the most efficient method for affiliate marketing. on Instagram.

Use a Linkable Instagram Gallery App:

Major e-commerce brands used Curalate's Link2Buy to set up a virtual shop with clickable Instagram posts on their profile. Over the years, other tools have come out that offer the same functionality, including the popular Linkin.bio service provided by the Instagram Later app. What happens is you set the link in your bio as the URL of your personalized Instagram gallery app. Once someone selects this, they will be taken to a screen of clickable Instagram posts that will lead to your affiliate links. You can find an example of what I'm talking about on my Linkin.bio page. You should be doing this on a cell phone to see what it would look like if you click my Instagram bio https://instagram.com / nealschaffer.

Insert an affiliate link as a swipe-up in Instagram stories (business accounts with only 10,000 followers):

If you happen to have a business account and 10,000 followers, you should see the option to add a swipe up link to your Instagram story so that your followers can easily access the website on the other side of your affiliate link. This is a good reason to upgrade to a corporate account, but the potential for less engagement due to how the pay-to-play social networking algorithms work prevents me from doing so.

Add the affiliate link to your photo, photo description, or Instagram story:

This is by far the least effective. However, if you use a URL shortener like Bl.ink and create a branded URL that is easy to remember and short enough to type in, some of your avid followers may take a screenshot of your photo or description and manually type the URL in your browser. If you can use a discount code instead of a URL, it will be easier for your followers to remember.

The benefits of Instagram affiliate marketing for brands

We can all imagine the benefits Instagram affiliate marketing bring to people, but what about the benefits of more affiliate relationships for the brand?

Increased brand awareness, engagement and follow-up on Instagram:

When a photo of a product or service is published on Instagram, the user (influencer) often marks the brand or service to which he belongs, or at least mentions the product and / or company. When this option is checked, people who see the message can interact with the message directly by opening, liking, or continuing to inquire about it. This is a win-win situation for both the marketer and the influencer as the incoming traffic increases and also creates a potential profit situation when a sale is made. In any case, it creates more brand awareness for the product - for free!

New relationships:

From a brand perspective, Instagram affiliate marketing can drive new relationships with influential users that only open up more and more opportunities. When a brand partners with an influencer and sales are generated, it opens up new channels for ongoing business, not one-off ads like most traditional ad campaigns. These business relationships can be of great benefit to both parties as brands are concerned about being featured on Instagram and the media, and users get both financial and PR benefits with these partnerships. It's that kind of collaboration that not every influencer wants, but there are many who do.

Increased sales:

With more than 1 billion users, Instagram gives affiliate marketing little choice to marketers not to take advantage of these partnerships. Today, Instagram has seen a significant increase in PR and marketing channels through the platform, with the sole purpose of promoting brands and various products. In this way, both the brand and a placement platform will see higher sales and greater engagement with followers than Instagram affiliate marketers.

At this point it seems worth explaining that in these partner partnerships the only thing that really matters is trust. Trust is required from your end of business with the other party in a partnership as well as for the trust that your brand / advertising platform has built through the user base. Social media influencers or PR firms are looking for value for a brand they promote as an Instagram affiliate marketer, while brands and products are only based on the level of trust they have in the other party. So what are the few "must haves" to look for in a partnership?

Which Instagram users and brands will be successful in Instagram affiliate marketing?

Those who offer brand value to their community:

For affiliate marketing on Instagram, both partners of the game must have a uniform brand value. The Instagram influencer who uses a product for advertising or shout -outs should be trusted by their many followers and have a positive impact on them. There shouldn't be a negative buzz about them when a user gets to know your brand through them. Likewise, the brand must have a competitive influence and be a product or service with an inherent value in the market.

Those who have a "good" following:

This is especially important for the influencer. There isn't an ideal number of followers to have, but a 'good' follower count would initially be in the range of 5,000-15,000, or at least 100 likes per photo in terms of engagement, provided your followers there are from real people and NOT from bots or paid followers. Even if an Instagram influencer doesn't have as many followers as others, the most important thing for those followers is to be actively engaged with the influencer's content and site. Known as micro influencers or even nano influencers (with less than 5,000 followers), these are of great importance to a new start up product that may not be able to work with macro influencers.

The Definitive Guide to Instagram Affiliate Marketing

Influencers from all industries try to monetize their influence on social media by doing affiliate marketing on Instagram. With Instagram becoming so popular around the world and with an active and engaged audience, Instagram's affiliate marketing is one of the main ways that influencers can monetize their social media.

For influencers who use Instagram as an affiliate marketer, the goal is to drive as much traffic as possible through their tracked links to the websites of their marketing partners. Because Instagram has a higher engagement than Tumblr, Twitter and Snapchat - or any other social network - Instagram's affiliate marketing offers a variety of options once you join, whether as a brand that wants to promote products or as a freelancer who wants to promote their services. If everyone is promoting on Instagram, you should too!

This post looks at Instagram affiliate marketing from both an influencer and brand perspective. Since this is going to be one of my longer sections, here is a quick bullet point summary so you know what to expect:

- How Instagram Affiliate Marketing Words - The Basics
- How can you promote links on Instagram if you can't create links on Instagram?
- The Benefits of Instagram Affiliate Marketing for Brands
- What types of Instagram users will be successful in Instagram affiliate marketing?
- Popular affiliate marketing marketplaces
- Understand FTC disclosure laws
- Switch from Instagram user to Instagram affiliate marketing
- How does Instagram affiliate marketing work?

It does this by building partnerships between a user who is the affiliate marketer and posting an introduction or promotion for a company's products or services on the marketer's website, in a social media post, or wherever . The affiliate marketer displays the product or service in their posts and earns a commission for every sale that can be attributed to their post, e.g. via a URL link that is provided with a unique affiliate code at the end of the article. When these affiliate promotions are done on Instagram we call it Instagram affiliate marketing, but affiliate marketing is clearly not limited to Instagram as a platform!

The brand that is being promoted and advertised wins the inherent interest of the customer, and the influencer profile that acts as an affiliate is used to attract its users to the advertised product. The influencer earns part of the sales from the advertised product. Therefore, it is mutually beneficial for the brand and the influencers to work together. This is why affiliate marketing is influencer marketing's new best friend!

How can affiliates promote links on Instagram if they cannot create links on Instagram?

I'll give some more specific advice for affiliate marketers later in this post, but one of the most direct questions you probably have is the comparison to blogs, Twitter, Facebook, LinkedIn, etc. Instagram doesn't let you post a link every time when you post a photo. How can affiliate marketers on Instagram get people to enter a link with their affiliate code in their browser and buy products? There are actually a few options once you get creative and think outside the box:

Partner link in your bio (permanent):

The obvious option is to use the link in your bio to direct people to the site. This works well when you keep promoting the same brand, product or link. Then you instruct users to click the link in their bio. Ideal if you are a brand ambassador and exclusive partner of a brand.

Partner link in your bio (semi-permanent):

If you want to promote a different product on each post, you can still use the link in your bio, but you should update it to the latest affiliate URL every time you post a new post. You can still tell users to click the link in your bio. However, should someone discover an older post promoting a different product, it will land on a different landing page. So this is not the most efficient method of affiliate marketing on Instagram.

Use a linkable Instagram Gallery app:

Major e-commerce brands used Curalate's Link2Buy to set up a virtual store with clickable Instagram posts on their profiles. Over the years, other tools have come out that offer the same functionality, including the popular Linkin.bio service later offered by the Instagram app. What happens is that you set the link in your bio as the URL of your personalized Instagram gallery app. Once someone selects this, they will be taken to a screen of clickable Instagram posts directing them to your affiliate links.

Insert the affiliate link as a swipe-up in Instagram Stories (business accounts with only 10,000 followers):

If you happen to have a business account and 10,000 followers, you should see the option to add a swipe up link to your Instagram story so that your followers can easily access the website on the other side of your affiliate link then visit it. This is a good reason to upgrade to a corporate account, but the potential for less engagement due to how the pay-to-play social networking algorithms work prevents me from doing so.

Add the affiliate link to your photo, photo description, or Instagram story:

This is by far the least effective. However, if you use a URL shortener like Bl.ink and create a branded URL that is easy to remember and short enough to type in, some of your avid followers may take a screenshot of your photo or description and manually type the URL in your browser. If you can use a discount code instead of a URL, it will be easier for your followers to remember.

The Benefits of Instagram Affiliate Marketing for Brands

We can all imagine the benefits Instagram affiliate marketing bring to people, but what about the benefits it brings to the brand in building more affiliate relationships?

Increased brand awareness, engagement and followers on Instagram:

When a photo of a product or service is posted on Instagram, the user (influencer) often marks the brand or service they belong to, or at least mentions the product and / or company. When checked, people who see the post can interact directly with the post by opening it, liking it, or asking further questions. This is a win-win situation for both the marketer and the influencer as the inbound traffic increases and a potential profit situation arises even if a sale occurs. Either way, it creates more brand awareness for the product - for free!

New relationships:

From a brand perspective, Instagram affiliate marketing can drive new relationships with influential users that open up more and more opportunities. When a brand partners with an influencer and sales are generated, it opens up new channels for ongoing business, not one-off ads like most traditional ad campaigns. These business relationships can be of great benefit to both parties as brands are concerned with being featured on Instagram and the media, and users get both financial and PR benefits with these partnerships. It's that kind of collaboration that not every influencer wants, but there are many who do.

Increased sales:

With more than 1 billion users, Instagram gives affiliate marketing little choice to marketers not to take advantage of these partnerships. Today, Instagram has seen a significant increase in PR and marketing channels through the platform, with the sole purpose of promoting brands and various products. In this way, both the brand and a placement platform will see higher sales and greater engagement with followers than Instagram affiliate marketers.

At this point, it seems worth pointing out that trust is of absolute importance in these partnerships. Trust is required for your end of business with the other party in a partnership, as well as the trust your brand / ad platform has built through its user base. Social media influencers or PR firms look for value in a brand they promote as an Instagram affiliate marketer, while brands and products are based solely on the trust they place in the other party. So what are the few "must-haves" to look for in a partnership?

Which Instagram users and brands will be successful in Instagram affiliate marketing?

Those who offer brand value to their community:

For affiliate marketing on Instagram, both partners must have a uniform brand value. The Instagram influencer who uses a product for advertising or shout outs should be trusted by their many followers and have a positive impact on them. There shouldn't be a negative buzz when a user gets to know your brand through them. Likewise, the brand must have a competitive influence and be a product or service with inherent value in the market.

Those who have a "good" following:

This is especially important for the influencer. There isn't an ideal number of followers you should have, but a "good" number of followers would be in the range of 5,000 to 15,000 to begin with, or in terms of engagement you want at least 100 times per photo, provided their fan base is real people and NOT bots or paid followers. Even if an Instagram influencer doesn't have as many followers as others, it is important that those followers actively engage with the influencer's content and page. Known as micro-influencers or nano-influencers (with fewer than 5,000 followers), these are of great importance to a new start up product that may not be able to afford to work with micro-influencers.

The ones that are relevant:

It is highly unlikely that a fashion and beauty influencer account will ever publish anything other than this topic in their portfolio. Hence, the mutual relevance between affiliate and brand for affiliate marketing on Instagram is of the utmost importance. This involves assessing whether your posts will fit into someone's feed and whether the audience will enjoy them. This requires a thorough search and review of all the details in every post the partner has written to determine relevance to a brand or product being marketed on their platform. For influencers, this means that you have to be just as picky about the products you represent to make them relevant to your community because you are what you tweet.

For individuals looking to get into affiliate marketing by becoming an online influencer and generating passive income through their followers, Instagram is a great platform connecting businesses with potential customers. But how do you find companies to work with? Let's take a look at some marketplaces that can make this easier.

CHAPTER EIGHT

TOP 16 AFFILIATE MARKETING NETWORKS

Affiliate Marketing is a very large industry and has become an important source of income on the Internet for many thousands of professional bloggers. As more and more online businesses get involved in affiliate marketing, bloggers like you and me have more and more opportunities to monetize their blog and ultimately create passive revenue streams.

With a variety of companies working directly with partners, most affiliate marketers use an affiliate marketing network to search for offers on their blogs. While these affiliate platforms cause a small reduction in the fees generated, they serve a valuable purpose in the affiliate marketing climate by:

Merging offers from different suppliers

Creating something like a search engine for affiliate marketers to find offers

Performing administrative tasks when running a connected network

In this chapter, I'll cover the 16 most popular affiliate marketing networks.

Partner window - (AWIN)

Formerly known as the Affiliate Window, officially named "AWIN" after the takeover of Zanox a few years ago, this network is said to work with more than 13,000 active advertisers and 100,000 publishers (affiliates). AWIN was founded in Germany and is mainly based in Europe (especially the UK), although the US network is growing rapidly. AWIN is currently active in 11 countries.

Founded in 2000, the company has since grown to become one of the most respected affiliate networks in the UK and the world. The company currently has more than 1,600 brands in 77 industries in 11 territories worldwide.

They also provide a simple, easy-to-use dashboard, as well as some useful tools that are sure to enhance your affiliate marketing campaigns.

Niche information:

AWIN is a very extensive connected network and works in all branches. That said, it is mostly focused on financial products, retail (fashion), sports, beauty, home and garden, and travel products.

Product types:

AWIN works with both digital and physical products, including some well-known retailers such as Hyatt, Etsy, AliExpress and HP (Hewlett-Packard).

Average commission percentage:

It all depends on the campaign and the merchant / advertiser. Pricing information is not displayed on the dashboard until the request to join AWIN is approved. AWIN offers are not tracked by Affscanner and OfferVault, so it is very difficult to measure commission rates and earnings potential without being a licensed publisher.

Cookie duration:

The duration of the cookie is determined by the advertiser.

Who is that for?

AWIN is probably best for seasoned partners who can get started right away without much guidance or feedback from the network. There is a $ 5 fee for applying for membership. If approved, the $ 5 will be added to your account. However, if your application is rejected, you will lose the $ 5 fee. AWIN operates worldwide, but mainly targets dealers in the UK and the EU.

AWIN has many powerful tools, including an Opportunity Marketplace, where you can promote sellers for unique one-time offers (such as sponsored posts). AWIN also has its own WordPress plugin that allows you to easily convert a link into a partner-specific link. There is also a Google Chrome extension.

AWIN includes Etsy as one of its sellers, making AWIN a great choice for bloggers looking to promote Etsy products.

A quick summary of the pros and cons of this program:

Advantages of AWIN:

- Pays twice a month (minimum $ 20).
- Real-time reports.
- Publishers / advertisers are heavily scrutinized.
- Very easy to use dashboard and many plugins available.
- 900 employees in 15 branches worldwide.

Disadvantages of AWIN:

- A $ 5 prepayment is required to register.
- Unapproved accounts will not be reimbursed the $ 5 fee.

ShareAsale

ShareASale is one of the largest affiliate networks and is now separate from AWIN. Around 4,000 dealers are listed on the ShareAsale platform, more than a thousand of which are exclusive to them. ShareASale publishes a large amount of data on each of their offers, including:

- Revenue per click
- Reversal rates

- Average sales volume
- Average commission

While these numbers are not guarantees of payouts that you can expect, they are certainly very helpful in evaluating a campaign.

Advantages of ShareASale:

Large partner network. More than 1,000 are exclusive among their 4,000 dealers.

Easy to compare offers. When trying to choose from the different offers available, ShareASale makes it really easy to judge the best, based on the metrics.

Fast payment cycle. ShareASale pays out on the 20th of each month, provided your account balance is over $ 50.

Flexoffers

Flexoffers is another great affiliate marketing network. They pay you (the partner) much faster than others in the industry. It has more than 10 years of experience in this field. While they don't offer anything that's either groundbreaking or revolutionary, they offer a solid selection of tools and features that are sure to help you in your campaigns. In addition to fast payouts, Flexoffers allows you to choose from thousands of affiliate programs to promote, offer different formats for content delivery and much more.

FlexOffers connects bloggers, content creators and other types of publishers with advertisers and brands with small, medium and large budgets.

You have thousands of different affiliate programs to choose from. They have broken these affiliate programs into dozens of broad and hundreds of subcategories, making it easier for the publisher to find exactly what fits their niche.

Flexoffers also has its own affiliate program which is a great way to earn additional commissions. If you refer someone to this network and they earn commission, you also recieve commission. You can earn up to 50% of all revenue generated by affiliates you refer to.

Advantages of FlexOffers:

- Share of sales. As I just said, if you refer someone to FlexOffers and they generate income, you get a discount on what they make.
- Dedicated affiliate manager. Many networks leave them to your own devices. Not FlexOffers. You will get your own affiliate manager to help you get the most out of your affiliate marketing efforts.
- Large number of affiliate programs. More than 15,000 partner programs to choose from and apply for.

Disadvantages of FlexOffers:

- Paypal is the only payment option for people based internationally (outside the US).

MaxBounty

Note: I have to include Maxbounty on this list as it is one of the largest affiliate networks out there. However, I do NOT recommend that you sign up.

My personal experience with MaxBounty has been one of frustration, anger, and stress. I sent tens of thousands of clicks to Maxbounty over the years only for them to close my affiliate account. This came with no warning, no email, nothing.

I sent them several emails asking "WTF is going on?". To date I have not received an answer.

So when you sign up for MaxBounty, be careful!

Here is the overview of MaxBounty ...

A relative newcomer to the connected space, MaxBounty was founded in Ottawa, Canada in 2004. MaxBounty claims to be the only affiliate network designed specifically for affiliates. MaxBounty is exclusively a CPA company (Cost Per Action / Acquisition) that does not deal with advertising banners and the like, but only with customer links that the publisher (blogger) selects where he wants to place them on his website.

Niche information:

Working in the corporate niche, MaxBounty claims to have 1,500+ active campaigns.

Product types:

MaxBounty works exclusively with digital products, usually by sending e-mails or registering for a newsletter. MaxBounty offers CPA, Pay-per-Call and CPL campaigns to choose from. MaxBounty operates in a wide variety of industries including market research, real estate, social games, finance, dating, and nutrition. However, it is primarily aimed at marketers looking to acquire new leads.

Average commission percentage:

The commission depends on the type of campaign. One look at their website shows everything from $ 2.50 to $ 85 per CPA, while other campaigns pay out a percentage of a sale. The transfer commission is five percent.

Cookie duration:

MaxBounty does not use cookies to track CPAs. The way MaxBounty works is that the partner sends a prospect to a specific landing page through an affiliate-specific link.

Who is that for?

MaxBounty tries to stay one step ahead by enforcing very strict anti-spam rules, sometimes in an annoying way. MaxBounty only works with digital products, not selling physical items. MaxBounty enables CPA promotions (and thus earning) via mobile devices.

As such, MaxBounty is probably best for medium to senior internet marketers who are confident in managing and sending traffic. If you are just starting out with the affiliate game, Max-Bounty is unlikely to make you much money.

MaxBounty is quite easy to understand and the dashboard is really well organized as it clearly lists the best offers for your niche.

A brief summary of the pros and cons of this program:

Benefits:

- $ 1,000 bonus for affiliates who earn $ 1,000 or more in the first three months.
- Weekly payments (minimum USD 50) by check, Paypal, Intercash, eCheck, ACH (direct deposit), bank transfer or Bitcoin.
- Has Worked with some well-known brands.
- User-friendly dashboard with handy sorting function for well-paid offers.

Downside:

- A large number of member companies reported negative experiences.
- Accounts are often terminated with little or no explanation.
- It can take a long time to obtain approval, including a voice call.

Trade doubler

Tradedoubler was founded in 1998 by two young North-European entrepreneurs. They have offices in the UK and several countries in Europe including Sweden, Germany, France, Poland and Spain. Its focus has always been on using technology to deliver smarter results to customers and affiliates. In 18 years, they have gathered an army of 180,000 active publishers and brought them into contact with more than 2,000 dealers in Europe and the UK. Many of these dealers are household names.

CJ Affiliate

CJ Affiliate is considered to be the largest online affiliate platform. If you've worked in affiliate marketing for a while, you have likely come across them

Almost every major retailer has their affiliate programs at CJ Affiliate (formerly Commission Junction), which makes them as close as possible to a one-stop shop in the affiliate marketing business. Most retailers have multiple ad sizes available to partners so that you have more control over the offers that you display on your blog.

With such a large number of advertisers on the CJ Affiliate platform, it is relatively easy to compare and segment different offers. It's also easy to find the affiliate tracking code to post on your blog. Once you have the right to advertise an offer, you can have many different offers on your website in a matter of hours.

Advantages of CJ.com:

- Large partner network. CJ Affiliate has over three thousand affiliates, many of whom have many creative formats and different affiliate link options.
- Reliable payments. They offer a net payment of $ 20 net, which means you will get your commission on time every month.
- Powerful reporting options. CJ Affiliate's reporting suite is quite impressive, which is a huge benefit for marketers who want to spend their time tweaking their sales performance.

Disadvantages of CJ.com:

- Steep learning curve. The reporting features are great, but quite difficult for beginners. You need to spend some time on the dashboard before you can comfortably navigate the report suite and then you can make the most of the tools on offer.
- Limited Customer Support. Given the large number of partners and resellers, it is understandable that customer support is very limited. However, it can be limiting to have only one contact form as the main method of contacting support.

Viglink

VigLink works a little differently from other affiliate programs as it is designed specifically for bloggers. Rather than having partners choose which merchants to work with, VigLink uses dynamic links that automatically change to work with merchants that VigLink has decided offer the highest call rates and / or commissions at any time.

In effect, VigLink acts as an intermediary between a publisher (blogger) and merchants by scanning the publisher's content and automatically creating links to publishers selected based on their payout / conversation rates "in real time". This makes VigLink a very simple affiliate program for publishers who prefer to focus on content rather than managing their affiliate links.

Niche information:

VigLinks works with all types of advertisers / sellers but categorizes them by "trends" or whatever is popular. It is important to note that this trending information comes from third party websites and not VigLink itself.

Product types:

VigLink is mostly about selling physical products, but also some digital products and services.

Average commission rate:

With VigLink partners can filter between CPC, CPA or CPA and CPA offers. The commission rates are set by the merchant, not VigLink.

Cookie duration:

This depends on the dealer and / or offer

Who is it for?

VigLink is an intermediate platform and can therefore serve as a back door for partners who have previously been prohibited / suspended from working with other partner programs such as Amazon. While you can select specific sellers or offers, VigLink can be set to work automatically by scanning your published content and dynamically generating affiliate links. This makes it a great choice for established content producers who are looking for an easier way to generate income through an affiliate program.

A quick summary of the pros and cons of this program:

Advantages of VigLink:

- Works well on websites / social media / apps.
- A page dashboard is very easy to use, yet powerful.
- Ideal for bloggers who want a more straightforward affiliate program.
- A great option for people who have been banned from Amazon or other affiliate programs.
- Can be set to update links dynamically to maximize your income.

Disadvantages of VigLink:

- Have to be approved individually by each dealer.
- The "automatic link creation" must be optimized (especially the WordPress plugin) in order to maximize the earning potential.
- Large payout differences between traders / offers.
- Only pays off once a month.
- VigLink takes a healthy portion of your commissions / earnings.

JVZoo

JVZoo was founded in 2011 and has since launched itself as one of the most popular affiliate programs in the market. JVZoo is unusual because neither publishers nor dealers (advertisers) have to incur any upfront costs. JVZoo's income is generated solely from the collection of fees (both from the dealer and from the affiliate) after a sale is completed. It is also uncommon for commissions to be paid "immediately" through PayPal, rather than once a week / fortnight / month as with other affiliate programs.

Niche information:

JVZoo works exclusively with digital products, mainly e-commerce, online courses and internet marketing offers. Since there is no limit to the number of links, buy buttons, or call-to-action on a website, JVZoo can sometimes be of somewhat poor quality, both in terms of deals and products. Still, it has proven to be a strong competitor to companies like ClickBank.

Product types:

JVZoo is primarily about selling online courses or getting people to share their information with marketing companies. However, JVZoo plays a leading role in introducing promotional items that appear every day.

Average commission percentage:

Commission rates vary by product / seller, but many of them offer returns of 50 percent or more.

Cookie duration:

Unlimited / Lifetime Cookies.

Who is that for?

JVZoo allows you to host and create landing pages on your own website. This is much better suited for professional marketers who want to flood the internet with offers, mostly for courses, to make money. You do not need your own website to participate in JVZoo. However, you need to know how to drive traffic to a landing or squeeze page to take advantage of a JVZoo affiliate.

The strength of JVZoo is that it gives seasoned marketers access to product launches and a variety of online courses, while also being able to set up sales funnels and custom landing pages. It is definitely not for someone looking to make money on a blog or make money by clicking through users and buying physical products. If you've built a strong marketing presence online, JVZoo might be the perfect choice.

A quick summary of the pros and cons of this program:

Advantages of JVzoo:

- Join for free and you can (later) qualify for instant pay-outs (PayPal).
- Ideal for bringing new product launches to market.
- You don't need your own website.
- You can (sometimes) recruit level two partners using the lifetime / unlimited cookies.
- Wide range of products and categories with detailed statistics on each program / retailer.

Disadvantages of JVZoo:

- Lots of videos and documentaries available but you have to pay to access them (one time fee).
- Many of the products are of relatively poor quality, if not genuine "spam".
- You must sell at least 50 products to receive instant PayPal withdrawals.
- The user dashboard is a little clunky and can sometimes fail.
- Many ads are hyperbolic and misleading.

Rakuten

Rakuten LinkShare is considered one of the oldest affiliate partner networks and is now much smaller than some of the larger players in the affiliate industry. There are some useful features in Rakuten LinkShare that set this platform apart from the rest.

For example, they have the ability to automatically scroll through the different banners for a product, which is a great advantage when optimizing your offers. Instead of having to manually choose which ad to show on your blog, LinkShare lets you rotate multiple versions with just a little code.

LinkShare also offers more flexible deep links to individual merchant landing pages so that the types of campaigns you run can be better customized.

LinkShare pros:

- Ad rotation. This seems like a minor feature, but it can make a significant difference in optimizing your ads.
- Deep link options. LinkShare allows you to choose the page you want to send your traffic to on your website, giving you more flexibility in promoting different partner offers.

LinkShare cons:

- A much smaller network. LinkShare has about 1,000 partners, so it is much smaller than larger networks such as ShareASale or CJ Affiliate.
- Unpredictable payments to affiliates. Rakuten LinkShare does not pay out to its affiliates until commissions are collected from their affiliates.

ClickBank

ClickBank is the God of affiliate marketing networks and has been around since the earliest days of the Internet. After Click-Bank (or "CB" for industry insiders) suffered from inferior products that were spam-proof in 2012, it has overhauled its verification process and created a much better dashboard.

There is a good reason why ClickBank is still a strong competitor even though it is more focused on digital products, of which, some can be of questionable quality. Yes, the review process is more professional these days, but it's still mostly focused on selling digital products, especially money making courses and the like. That said, there are some very high quality products on offer, and few affiliate programs are bigger than ClickBank, especially when it comes to selling books (mostly digital).

Niche information:

Until now, ClickBank has mainly focused on digital products, especially marketing courses, but now it has expanded its offering significantly to include physical goods.

Product types:

ClickBank's focus is more on niche courses, e-books, and on-line courses, although they have also expanded to include some physical goods.

Average commission percentage:

Up to 75%.

Cookie duration:

The duration of the cookies depends on the product, but none of them are unlimited / lifelong.

Who is it for?

Participation in ClickBank is free and the approval process is almost automatic. Hence, it is a great choice for first-time affiliate users. ClickBank has a variety of information, including frequently asked questions (FAQs), how-tos, and videos. Therefore, the entry barrier is quite low. There is also a (paid) program called ClickBank University, with courses and help from experienced marketers.

There is also a second tier program called the "Joint Venture Program" that allows you to work with ClickBank partners. This is a kind of second tier affiliate program. There is an approval process for this, but the commissions are higher. ClickBank is ideally positioned for publishers (bloggers) operating in smaller niches.

A quick summary of the pros and cons of this program:

Pros:

- Weekly payouts with many different payout options.
- The joint venture program offers even higher revenues. One of the largest and most robust affiliate programs available.

- ClickBank offers a 60-day, no-questions-asked, money-back guarantee on ALL products.
- Immediate approval process.

Cons:

- The refund policy improves conversion rates, but it can eat up your income.
- Strong competition from other partners selling the same products.
- Some digital products sold are of very poor quality.
- The first payments are only made by check. Only after a minimum number of sales can you receive payouts via bank transfer or PayPal.
- Limited choice of physical products.

Target partner

As with Amazon, Target's partner program is designed to help bloggers and publishers monetize the sale of Target (the brick and mortar retailer)'s products. Since most Americans know and trust Target, the affiliate program can be very lucrative for well-positioned content creators.

Niche Information:

This program only works with physical products sold by Target Stores.

Product types:

Anything sold on Target's website.

Average commission percentage:

The commissions are relatively low and a maximum of eight percent.

Cookie duration:

Cookies expire after seven days.

Who is it for?

Since Target is the second largest retailer in the United States, the affiliate program primarily targets American bloggers or publishers who can direct visitors to relevant products. In general, the program works in the same way as Amazon's in that publishers (bloggers) receive a small commission on the sale, but Target's massive product base (over a million items) and high brand awareness make their affiliate program a great option for influencers.

However, generating income through Target Partners requires some work. Cookies expire in just seven days and the commissions can be as low as one percent. So you need a high traffic website to be able to make big bucks on this program. Because of Target's popular brand reputation and extensive catalog, relevant product links can be big earners for established influencers.

A quick summary of the pros and cons of this program:

Advantages:

- Very trustworthy brand.
- Huge product catalog (over a million)
- Great alternative to Amazon's affiliate program.
- Established influencers can make a lot of money.
- You will be paid for EVERY purchase made on Target (sent through your link), not just for the specified product.

Disadvantages:

- The commission rates are quite low, especially for small sellers.
- Oddly enough, some product categories have no commission at all.
- The conversion rates are lower than on Amazon.
- Only suitable for websites with a predominantly American audience
- Only four main categories have commission rates comparable or higher than Amazon.

SkimLinks

SkimLinks works similarly to VigLinks in that it is designed for bloggers who don't want to do a lot of practical work to join an affiliate program. SkimLinks is similar to VigLinks because it uses a script or plugin to create dynamic links in your content and send visitors to higher paying avilable offers. SkimLinks claims to work with over 24,000 sellers / advertisers.

One big difference between SkimLinks and VigLinks, however, is that once approved by the company, you can work with any reseller or program on their platform. SkimLinks has also released a whitepaper discussing the partnership with Buzzfeed, which gives SkimLinks a lot of credibility. SkimLinks also has a higher number of verified dealers called "Preferred Partners" and "VIP", both of which pay higher commissions than standard dealers.

Niche information:

SkimLinks works with a wide variety of products, but focuses more on physical items.

Product types:

SkimLinks works with both physical and digital products. However, it seems to have a stronger focus on physical products, including fashion (clothing) from famous brands and many products from Amazon, Target and eBay.

Average commission percentage:

Commission rates vary depending on the retailer, but the best commissions (up to 100 percent) are offered by the 400+ members of their Preferred Partner and VIP programs.

Cookie duration:

The duration depends on the dealer.

Who is it for?

SkimLinks is primarily aimed at established content producers (bloggers) who want to monetize their content. With a powerful WordPress plugin and scripts for almost any website type, setting up SkimLinks is very easy. And since you can access all the offers on their platform after approval, this network is great for affiliates who don't want to spend a lot of time on settings and other fine-tuning.

SkimLinks is probably best for bloggers who want to write content through the affiliate link instead of adding affiliate links to existing products. SkimLinks has many tools for comparing commission rates and offers to customize your content and optimize your income. Another nice thing about SkimLinks is that it has a lot of products for non-US developers, including popular UK brands like John Lewis and Tesco.

A quick summary of the pros and cons of this program:

Pros:

- Great customer service.
- Email notifications for sellers whom you have marked as favorites.
- Very easy integration into your existing website.
- Powerful and user-friendly interface.
- Amazon and Ebay links are automatically directed to the correct region.

Cons:

- Skimlinks are free to use, but 25 percent of all commissions are charged.
- Only pays off once a month.
- Slightly limited number of sellers / advertisers.
- Some websites load slower after adding SkimLinks code.

Warrior Plus

The Warrior Plus website and user interface looks like it used to, but Warrior Plus is a strong competitor in promoting online courses and marketing programs to make money. Where Warrior Plus excels is the instant payments (via PayPal) and payouts on all products in the sales funnel.

Because product reviews (including payback rates) take a lot of time and effort, Warrior Plus is best for experienced marketers looking to earn commissions on a wide variety of programs.

Niche information

Warrior Plus (or Warrior + as it is known in some quarters) is devoted entirely to internet marketing.

Product types

The only products for sale through Warrior Plus are digital products, including one-time offers and "free" courses offered in exchange for contact information. Most Warrior Plus products are money making courses (known in the industry as MMO / BizOpp).

Average commission percentage

Commission rates vary widely depending on the product.

Cookie duration

The duration of the cookies depends on the product.

Who is it for?

This network is ideal for experienced online marketers who want to earn commissions on (different) internet marketing offers. Warrior Plus's clunky user interface and sheer number of (often) inferior products make it best suited for seasoned partners who have advanced methods of directing traffic to specific links.

A quick summary of the pros and cons of this program:

Pros:

- Simple and free approval process.
- Large number of (digital) products on offer.
- Very transparent operation and high commissions for some products.
- Useful statistics on suppliers.
- Paypal direct withdrawals or withdrawals via Stripe.

Cons:

- Requires approval from each vendor, and this can be very time consuming (even it is more professional).
- Sells a large number of low quality products.

- Refunds can devour your income.
- You must sell five times before you can receive your first payout
- Lack of transparency / information on some products.

Peerfly

Peerfly is a CPA network with an extensive list of digital and physical products. This affiliate network stands out from its competitors because it offers a multi-level affiliate program that allows you to earn 5% from every sale your secondary affiliates makes in their first year.

Although PeerFly has a dynamic and well-designed website, PeerFly has a limited selection of offers (approximately 8,000) at any given time. On the plus side, it offers good commission / payout rates, FAQs and educational information, and regular contests and reward programs that can significantly increase your bottom line. Based on online customer ratings, it enjoys a very high reputation among the participating affiliates.

Niche information:

PeerFly offers a variety of products, but most of them are mostly digital. Even so, PeerFly has won some large customers including Target, CBS, and Fiverr.

Product types:

Mainly digital, but also many physical products.

Average commission:

Depends on the dealer.

Cookie duration:

Depends on the product.

Who is it for?

PeerFly is intended for legitimate partners who do not mind undergoing the rigorous application process. PeerFly has spent a lot of time setting up the dashboard and website to be very intuitive and easy to use. So once you are "in", things work very smoothly.

PeerFly currently has a limited number of products, but they are hugely dynamic and growing by leaps and bounds. Their payout rates are not spectacular, but everything is upfront and transparent, and partner satisfaction is very high. PeerFly is perfect for authentic marketers who want to bring high quality products to their visitors instead of getting rich. Fast and opaque deals.

PeerFly's second tier affiliate program means that established influencers can earn a great deal.

A quick summary of the pros and cons of this program:

Pros:

- Very high degree of satisfaction among the affiliated companies.
- Large UX / UI.

- Careful screening ensures little or no spam or fake products.
- Super easy setup and powerful dashboard.
- Withdrawal every 7./15/30 days via PayPal, Amazon gift cards, checks, Payoneer, Bitcoin or bank transfer.

Cons:

- The minimum payout is $ 50.
- Only 15 employees.
- Limited number of products.
- Strict application process.
- Customer service can be very slow and there is a limited amount of frequently asked questions / educational information on their website.

LinkConnector

LinkConnector struggled to stand out from the package but was able to land some exclusive deals with well-known brands including Writer's Digest, Disney Store, Ironman, Hats.com and Everly. Thanks to the strictly controlled verification process for both retailers / advertisers and affiliated companies / publishers, you can always rely on the quality of the products on offer.

However, LinkConnector's platform looks dated and feels pretty clumsy. Their dashboards also make it difficult to find "hot" products or compare conversion rates, leaving partners a little in the dark about which products to choose. Ironically, even though their website quality is low, they offer one of the best customer services in the affiliate network's world.

Niche information:

LinkConnector works with a variety of products offered as CPA (Click Per Action), CPS (Click Per Second), PPC (Pay Per Call), and PPL (Pay Per Lead).

Product types:

LinkConnector's products are roughly evenly split between digital and physical products. Most digital products are e-commerce rather than e-books or online courses.

Average commission:

The commission rates depend on the seller.

Cookie duration:

The duration of the cookie depends on the seller.

Who is it for?

LinkConnector is a mixed bag, so it is probably best for seasoned partners who are disaffected with other networks and want to expand. LinkConnector's bizarre mix of high quality products and a low quality dashboard makes it difficult to really gauge profitability, but their exclusive offers with some vendors can make it a real home run for publishers working in certain niches.

LinkConnector requires a very strict and lengthy verification process. So you need to prove you have a quality website and an established audience before being accepted. Despite its somewhat schizophrenic approach, LinkConnector has some very lucky long-term affiliates. And their "bare links" allow a direct link to the sales page without having to be redirected through LinkConnector, which gives your website an SEO boost.

This is probably best for established influencers who work in the home niches, apparel, and fashion, or those who can drive traffic to CPA websites for promotions such as filling out contact information forms or phone calls.

A brief summary of the pros and cons of this program:

Pros:

- Exclusive access to some well-known brands.
- Very high quality products that are heavily assessed.
- Good customer service.
- Uses private voucher codes that prevents them from being "hijacked".
- Provides "naked links" that do not require redirection through the LinkConnector website. This is a huge SEO boost.

Cons:

- Poorly designed website and dashboard.
- Very strict screening process (up to 60 percent of applicants are rejected).

- The dealer can determine where the links appear.
- Limited choice of physical products.
- Highly inclined to traders via traders.

AvanGate (2Checkout)

AvanGate is now officially known as 2Checkout, which has caused a lot of confusion for many traders. What's more confusing is that the original Avangate name now refers to a payment processor, while 2Checkout is the affiliate program. However, 2Checkout uses AvanGate to process all withdrawals, making 2Checkout a subsidiary of Avangate.

2Checkout, the partner program, focuses solely on the sale of software and other digital goods as opposed to registrations, form filling or online courses. 2Checkout sells more than 22,000 different software products from various well-known companies, including Kaspersky, Hewlett-Packard and BitDefender.

Niche information:

2Checkout works exclusively with digital products, mainly software, e-commerce and SaaS.

Product types:

2Checkout deals exclusively with software, digital products and SaaS solutions (Software as a Service).

Average commission rate:

The commission rates vary depending on the product, but are between 25 and 80 percent.

Cookie duration:

Cookies expire after 120 days.

Who is it for?

Since 2Checkout only sells software and digital products, it is best suited for established influencers whose target audience is interested in buying products in this niche. While you won't find any physical products for sale, 2Checkout is likely to be the industry leader in selling software of any kind, including very specific use case elements (e.g. software that can convert Microsoft Word documents to PDF).

Unfortunately, the 2Checkout dashboard is somewhat limited in size, which makes it difficult to get statistics on the conversion rate or to sort out commission payouts. The solution is to go to the Avangate store, which lists the top selling products, and then find them on the affiliate dashboard. However, 2Checkout offers products from more than 4,000 different suppliers, making it the leading networked network for software and digital products.

With recent business changes and the transformation of 2Checkout into a larger payment processing and e-commerce company, the Affiliate Program can feel a little neglected at times. The ability to generate custom coupon codes and the extensive knowledge base make 2Checkout a good option for seasoned partners with an established user base. The first time you enter the partner field, 2Checkout may not be where you want to start.

A quick summary of the pros and cons of this program:

Pros:

- An industry leader in affiliate sales for software and SaaS products.
- Long cookie duration (120 days).
- Can create unique vouchers.
- Very generous commission rates.
- Payment by PayPal, direct deposit or a branded Master-Card (Avangate).

Cons:

- Minimum withdrawal of USD 100.
- The dashboard has limited search / sort options.
- Reports contain some useful details.
- Very high number of dissatisfied customers, many of whom are annoyed by unexpected or unauthorized charges.
- Occasional poor customer service.

CHAPTER NINE

22 COMMON AFFILIATE MARKETING MISTAKES YOU NEED TO AVOID

If you're thinking about beginning your affiliate marketing business, you are probably a bit scared of all the possible beginner mistakes in affiliate marketing.

Or maybe you have already started and fear that you are doing something wrong.

Yes? Don't worry, I'm here to help.

Let's take a look at the 22 Most Common Affiliate Marketing Mistakes to Avoid.

1. Trying to make money right away

Look:

Affiliate marketing is not something that you can get rich with right away.

Whatever you do, and however you do it, you will never make any money with affiliate marketing in the near future. It is impossible. Why?

Well, for a couple of reasons:

- You have no connections
- You have no or very little traffic
- You have little content
- You don't know much about how you can make money from affiliate marketing
- and nobody trusts or knows you (yet)

When this comes to your mind, you and your affiliate / niche website will really stand a chance of success.

What you should do:

Don't waste time flooding your website with your affiliate links OR participating in every affiliate program you come across OR promoting any high-ticket product. You need to focus on the more important things first.

I am not saying that making money is not important. I'm saying it is not that important to begin with. OK?

First, work on these three things:

Write great content

Get traffic

Email collection (we'll come back to this in a moment)

If you have all of these 3 settings first, you can make money for a long time.

2. Not Collecting Email subscibers From The Beginning

Here's one that 90% of newbies do. I was one of them. I didn't start making my list or about 7-8 months.

If you ask a seasoned (or even advanced) blogger, online marketer, or online business owner, what is the most important asset you could ever have (for your website)? It will be not collecting email subscibers from the beginning. I guarantee that at least 90% of them will provide a list of active email subscribers. Why is it important to have a list of email subscribers?

For many reasons:

A. You get more traffic

Let's say you have a loyal list of 1,500 subscribers and you just released a 4,000-word epic beast.

You can send them an email to let them know. And I guarantee that at least 30% of them will read your post and at least half of it will be shared on social media. This is better than waiting (and praying) for your first Google rank.

B. If Google gives you a penalty (or if they get destroyed out of the blue), you still have your list

Give it a try: Let's say you have about 2,500 monthly Google Search visits and about 3,000 subscribers.

Google then introduces one of its algorithm updates. You are hit for performing unreliable link building. You lose your position on the first page and 100% of your search traffic. It would be the end of the world for you.

The same thing would happen if someone dropped an atomic bomb on Google. However, you still have the email addresses of 3,000 people who love your content.

Every time you post a new message, you can email it and still have at least 1,000 eyes on your content. And there's still a high chance they'll share it, which could mean a lot more traffic on social media. And maybe some of them are subscribed to your list. See?

C. More subscribers = more visitors = more sales

For example, with a loyal list of 5,000 email subscribers, you can separate an online business or blog from a blog with a monthly price of $ 500 and a blog with a monthly price of more than $ 5,000. Partners who don't start making their lists early will make a mistake.

What you should do:

Now build your list. I will help you on your way.

Here's what to do (if you're using the WordPress platform, if not, adapt this information to your website builder as you can):

1) Sign up for an email marketing service:

There are a few to choose from, all of them are great. Here are some of the most popular:

- MailChimp - This is the one I'm using now. It's free for up to 2000 subscribers (I'll probably switch services once I'm over 2000).
- Aweber - starting at $ 19 per month for up to 500 sub-scribers (offers a 30-day free trial)
- Getresponse - Starts at $ 15 per month for up to 1,500 subscribers

I'm using Mailchimp (because it's free). So create your account. They have all the directions to help you out.

2) Create a new email list:

I've put together a number of screenshots to make it easier for you to follow. What to do: You will be redirected to a page where you need to fill out the form details:

Done. You now have a new list.

3) Install or upload a sign up form plugin:

There are many WordPress login form plugins to choose from. Here are some that I think you'll want:

- MailChimp for WP - The Lite version is free and simple. However, there are no customizable functions

- WP subscription - This is the free version of the version you see on this site.
- MailMunch - Increase Your Email Subscribers - Another free sign-up form plugin.
- Optin forms from Codeleon (Boris Beo) - This is great. And it is 100% free!

I'll be using Codeleon's Optin Forms for my example because it's cool (I recommend it too!). So open a new tab and login to your wp-admin area. Then go to - Plug-ins> Add New and search for "Registration forms". Now click on the Install button and activate the plugin. Now you are on the page: leave it there and return to the MailChimp tab.

4) Connect your email service with the right plugin:

For this part, you will need to go to your email service account and get what's called an API key or list ID. You need your list ID for the Optin Forms plugin.

You can find the instructions on the plugin page. You need to click the question mark next to the form action URL. The instructions on the plugin page may be a bit difficult to follow as MailChimp has since updated the design.

But don't worry, here's what to do:

- First you need to click on Registration forms.
- Then Embedded Forms> Select.
- When you are on the embedded form page, click Naked.
- Then get your list ID here.

In my experience, you can't get the list Id itself because the whole thing is copied. If this happens to you, all you have to do is open a Word document, paste everything there and copy your list ID.

Okay, now go back to the plugin page and paste your list ID where the form action url is. Hit the Save Changes button and you're done. Now you are ready ...

5) Customize your registration form:

OKAY. You are now done with the setup and can customize your registration form. There are 5 designs/template of opt-in forms you can choose from.

So choose one that fits the theme of your website.

There are also other customizable options:

- Choose the colors
- Select the required fields (eg first name).
- Choose whether or not to open it in a new window
- Select where you want the message to be published (for example, at the start or the end of a message).

Make sure it suits you, okay? And put the registration form at the end of your posts (under the form entry tab). Finished.

Now is the time to try and get some email addresses.

3. Pick a niche they are not interested in

This is one of the worst mistakes you could ever make in affiliate marketing. Why?

Well, because you don't really enjoy talking or writing about the subject. I'll give you an example ...

When I first started this whole affiliate and niche marketing thing, the first niche I wanted to look at was the video game niche. But since that was way too broad for a beginner, I went with custom / modified Xbox controllers. Was that a good (profitable) niche? Yes. It's actually still like that.

The controllers cost between $ 50 and $ 250 with a commission of 10 to 30 percent. And ... there are many people who are interested in them. So what happened to me?

Although I was very interested in Xbox games, I hardly had any in the controllers. Not enough to find out more about it. I had only written 2 blog posts and 4 pages. They were all 500 words or less. There is not much quality, is there?

After about a few months, I stopped updating it. Now it is literally just a blank white page.

What to do: Pick a niche you are interested in. At least a little. Enough to enjoy reading and writing about his topics.

I'm talking about the 5 questions to ask yourself on the Simple Online Cash Money blog. If you're unsure of how to pick a niche, this is a good place to take a look.

4. Publication of very low quality and illegible content

Posting 150-word product reviews and 400-word tutorials that don't even show the reader how to do something is NOT going to do your blog any good.

Even a message with a 1,500 word list may not help if it is not formatted properly. In other words, writing large blocks of text is not a good idea.

No bulleted lists, no images, no headings (h2, h3 tags), no bold or italic fonts, and a boring paragraph, wow! No wonder no one has read my content.

What To Do: You should start writing content that can help someone. And I mean really helping someone.

Suppose you want to write a message about changing tires.

Your headline would be something like this:

How to change a tire in less than 15 minutes

Replace your tire in 5 minutes by following these 4 steps

The Lazy Man's Guide to Changing Flat Tires

And then you would write your template like this:

- Introduction
- Step 1: Prepare your tools
- Step 2: set up the socket
- Step 3: Remove the nuts / bolts

- Step 4: replace the tire
- Step 5: Tighten the nuts / bolts
- Conclusion

Now you can write down your concept. You also need to make your message easy to read.

You can do this by:

- Using short and simple words
- Using short paragraphs (1-4 sentences).
- Using images and screenshots
- Using bold and italics
- Using heading tags
- Using bulleted lists

5. Do not write product reviews

Product reviews are an important part of an affiliate marketing website. Why? Because people looking for product reviews likely have their credit cards ready.

Partners who do not rate products in their niche are missing out on internet users ready to buy.

Reviews are also the most important type of content you could ever create on your affiliate website. So, you need to start posting reviews.

This is how I do it:

1) Choose a product:

A product listed on your blog must fall into one of the following categories:

- 100% scam: so you can send readers your referral
- Another good product so you can send readers your recommendation
- 100% Legitimate - so you can send readers to the check-out page through your affiliate link
- To find products in your niche, you can google:
- Best (your niche) - Example: The best diet supplements for weight loss
- Best (your niche) products - for example: The best products for weight loss
- (your niche) - Example: How men can lose weight quickly
- (your niche) products - eg Weight loss products
- (your niche) companies - for example: weight loss companies
- Buy (your niche product) - Example: Buy a weight loss supplement

Or you can browse affiliate programs such as:

- Amazon
- Shareasale
- Clickbank

You can also go to shops with a wide variety of products. For example Walmart.

2) Search for a keyword:

Many SEOs have said that keyword research is the first step to getting ranked in Google. Is it true? Of course.

For this step, you will need to switch to a keyword tool. You can use one of the following options:

- Google Keyword Planner: all you need is a Google account.
- KeywordTool.io: free
- KW Finder: it gives you 5 free searches per day
- Jaaxy: Create a free account and get your first 30 free searches

When you get to the Keyword Tool page, a search bar appears. Enter the product name here. When you do this, keyword terms such as "review" and "work" will appear in the results.

You can also use a keyword phrase that the internet user will answer. For example, you are in the weight loss niche, and you are reviewing a product that is said to be real business. You can use terms like: best pill for weight loss, lose weight fast or burn fat without exercising.

This is only possible if: it makes sense, there are a large number of monthly searches and the product is legitimate.

3) Find out about the product

Now is the time to learn as much as possible about the product you have chosen. Information can be found on the product sales pages. Other reviews are done by other bloggers/marketers.

You can do this with a few Google searches:

- (product name) rating
- (Product Name) Reviews
- What is (product name)
- Buy (product name)
- 4) Write down your template:
- Here is the typical product review template:
- (preface)
- What is? / Product overview
- Advantages and disadvantages
- Characteristics
- The pricing
- Conclusion

5) Leave your trip:

Your writing begins here. Since you've written a template, writing the actual review is 10x easier.

Tip: aim for at least 1000 words.

6) optimize for search engines (Google):

Search engine traffic is probably the number one source of traffic for your reviews.

In fact, it's probably the only source of traffic. The optimization for the search is therefore very important.

Here's what you need to do: First, make sure your target keyword is in the right places:

- In your title / headline
- In your first 100 words or so
- In the main part of your review (1-10 times)
- In the alt tag of your picture

Then you need to add some links. Internally and externally. But make sure it makes sense. I usually go for at least 2 of each:

- 2 links pointing to your older posts / reviews.
- 2 links that refer to articles / pages on government websites.

Here are some other things you can do:

- Use LSI / related keywords
- Use pictures
- Make a long copy

7) Proofreading. To edit. Publish:

After you've finished writing your review and optimizing it for the search engines, it's time to read your paper. I usually read it slowly and when I see something that needs to be changed I read it again until I think it's perfect. Like this:

- Read the message.
- See Errors, Correcting Errors and then reading on.
- Read the message again (from above).

I'll go into more detail on writing reviews later on, so if you need more help, be sure to read this.

6. Relying Heavily on Google Search Traffic

The special thing about Google: they don't index or review websites that are a few days old. They don't even rank pages in the top 10 if they are only a few weeks old.

How am I supposed to know? From personal experience.

I started this site last January. My first message was over 3,000 words long. My second, third, fourth, and fifth posts were between 1,200 and 2,500 words long, so guess what, none of them were in the top 100 Google results.

This happened for two reasons:

- I had no authority in my niche (meaning my website was too new and I was a nobody)
- The keywords I focused on were a bit too competitive

The first thing you need is patience. OK? Second, you need to set up your website for SEO (Search Engine Optimization). Third, you should write high-quality blog posts targeting long-tail keywords. Finally, you need to research other traffic sources (e.g. social media).

Flooding your posts with affiliate links. This is bad for three reasons:

- It does not help the reader
- Google doesn't like too many affiliate links in a single post or page, and they don't look professional (youraffiliatelink.com?aaid193729product)
- Place your affiliate links strategically. The following must be done:
- Place it somewhere in the body once or twice
- Place it once after every other subhead
- Put it once at the end of the post / review (your call to action).
- And use an affiliate link cloaker (we'll get to that in a moment).

8. Do not camouflage your affiliate links

You know what an affiliate link looks like, right? Ugly. Just ugly. Here's an example: Affiliatelink.com?a_id-718473810

Having a few of these in one post would look awful and unprofessional.

Dress up your affiliate links. Change this: product-owner.com?a_aid123 to: yourdomain.com/product name.

You can do this with a (WordPress) plugin. I recommend Pretty Link. It's free and easy.

How to use it:

1. Install the plugin: First you have to login to your wp-admin. Then go to Plugin> Add New, look for the pretty link, install and enable it.
2. Create a "good link": On the plugin page and in the left menu there is a link "add new".
3. Create your new beautiful link: Paste your affiliate link where the destination url is. Then the snail and the title ...

The snail should be something like:

/ product name
/ product
/ buy product
/ go product

Make sure it includes the name of the product. Use the name of the product for the title and select the Follow this link check box in the Options tab. Then hit the Create button and you are done.

No need to worry about the Advanced tab or the class action.

4. add your "nice link" to your posts:
Now all of your affiliate links will look professional and beautiful.
A good alternative is the ThirstyAffiliates plug-in. It's a little more advanced than the Pretty Link plugin, however.

9. Participate in every affiliate program you see

Do you know why this is a mistake? Because new affiliate sites have no traffic. So it really doesn't make sense.

In addition, different products (and programs) can be difficult to promote. For an affiliate site to work, there must only be 1 or 2 products that are highly recommended by the affiliate. This is a great way to drive traffic from your posts to product review.

If you are doing this for the long run then you should only focus on 1, maybe 2 affiliate programs.

10. Bullshitting About Scammy Products

I admit - I always did this when I started my first niche affiliate website. Big mistake. Maybe that's why the website is no longer active.

Do you want to know what happened? I was promoting this product with a price of $ 150 and a 40% commission.

Those are pretty good numbers, aren't they? Yes. But something wasn't right - there were hundreds of negative customer reviews. It had 5 stars. But I couldn't resist.

And since I made it look like a quality product, I was able to generate some sales - about 15 (I only had 100 page views at the time).

After about a week (when the customers got their orders) I got a bunch of crazy people who emailed me and commented on my blog. Big regret.

I strongly advise against doing what I did.

What should you do? It's easy. Never do what I did. You lose confidence and some potential repeat visitors. Always give them the truth.

If you're reviewing a bad product, let your readers know it's a bad product. You can then send them to a review of a quality product. Do you need help writing product reviews? No problem.

11. Do not test the recommended products

Look: I'm not saying you should buy and try every product you review. I say you should test the products you promote. This way, you can give your readers a rating that is 100% factual. You can also answer all their questions with correct answers.

It's a win-win situation in that they win because they get high quality products from you, and you win because they trust you.

Test the product you are promoting. Period.

12. Sell! Sell! And Sell!

Here's what I'm talking about: Suppose you're promoting the Hydroxycut Dietary Supplement for Weight Loss. You write your main review and direct readers to the sales / checkout page. And then write a blog post promoting your review. And then another and another.

Then write a blog post promoting the product and a few more, then another evaluation.

That's a total of 8 posts, all of which have exactly the same content.

Since every post is about how awesome Hydroxycut is, there is nothing else to read. Why would someone come back and want to read the same thing over and over again? I know I wouldn't.

What you should do Don't create messages that are essentially the same thing: advertisements.

13. Do not do their job

I know staying motivated and continuing to work on your website is difficult. It happens. I was there. Well, actually I still am.

There are times when I travel for days without logging into my website. And do you know what happens when you are not working on your website? Nothing.

You have to work every day. I know it's harder than it sounds, but if you want to be a successful affiliate marketer, you have to be disciplined. You have to be motivated.

14. Spamming your affiliate links on social networks and advertising networks

Posting a link on Facebook groups, ad networks, etc. is an enormous waste of time.

Nobody will ever click on your affiliate link, especially not on social media because they are strangers to you. And it looks spammy.

Have you been on Facebook groups Many of them are inundated with offers from people and affiliate links. Oh, and do you know why they post on FB groups?

Because they are told ... by the "gurus" who "teach" them how to use the internet to make money.

How am I supposed to know? That's exactly what I did a year ago.

I paid nearly $ 100 a month to an online business adversary for 5 months to make money online and get access to their affiliate program. And all I did was post my affiliate link on some FB groups. And do you know how many recommendations I made? ONE. And he was a buddy (we hardly talk anymore, probably because he thinks I've been kidding him).

So social media groups are a bad idea if you are a newbie.

What should you do? Stick to your blog / website. Don't waste time posting your affiliate links on social media groups and advertising networks.

The only thing I would recommend you do on Facebook / social media is to create your own group that caters to your niche:

For example, if you're in the gaming niche, create a Facebook group that's all about gaming. Here you can share your content, post offers or sales and even share your affiliate links from time to time.

15. Try to be a super partner

By that I mean this: A man named Mr. John wants to make money on the internet.

So he builds a website that focuses on the weight loss niche (which is very competitive).

He sets up his website, writes a few posts and believes he will make money quickly because he thinks he has his website ready.

So he builds another website. This time in the gaming niche. Same thing here - done a few posts. Then he builds a few more.

Now he thinks he is a true affiliate marketer expert - a super affiliate. Do you think Mr. John made money? No

Mr. John got very angry a few weeks after he "finished" his blogs. And finally he said "Fuck it!" Okay. I was actually "Mr. John."

Yes. I am an idiot.

What you should do…. Don't act like Mr. John (or … me). Stick to one project. And if you're good at writing content, building websites, and more, you can work on new projects.

Cool? Cool.

16. Promote every $ 1,000 product they see

If you do this now, chances are you will hardly generate any affiliate sales. In fact, you probably aren't even making money.

Why? Maybe your target audience doesn't have deep pockets.

Another reason could be that you didn't set your posts / reviews as they should be. And do I set up my reviews on my other website. Yes.

The product I'm promoting is only $ 47 and 50% goes to me. And it's a member product where members pay monthly. That means I get a commission every month that customers keep paying. In addition, it is a real quality product.

So if you are only promoting products with high prices, I recommend stopping.

What you should do You don't have to promote high-ticket products to make good money. If you can make around $ 5 to $ 25 per sale (commission), that's more than enough to make $ 500 a month.

So focus on the quality of the product. Not how much it costs.

17. Your sidebars, headers, and footers are flooded with banner ads

This is one of the biggest mistakes a blogger or affiliate can ever make. Why?

First, it can be difficult to navigate or look around. Second, it looks really unprofessional.

Do you know what will happen when you do this? Internet users who are real people hit the back button before they can even say hello.

What you should do

You don't have to worry about ads for the first few weeks of your blog. Wait until you have published at least 10 or even 20 quality posts. And then you can run an ad once or twice in your main sidebar.

18. Promote products that have nothing to do with their niche

This is a mistake that many beginners make.

Let me give you an example of this: Mr. Joe J. Joseph is starting a blog for those looking for premium WordPress themes. So he publishes around 20 posts and reviews. Then he slowly gets bored. Therefore, he is writing a contribution to the promotion of online marketing training.

"WTF? I thought that was a WP-themed page!"

Then he does it again. This time he's trying to sell a keyword research tool. And then another.

"Okay, that's not so bad" you might think. Well, it is.

Here's the deal: Joe's audience is made up of website owners interested in premium WordPress themes, right? These people are likely to be successful bloggers, marketers, and small businesses.

Why would a successful blogger care about an online marketing course? Understood?

What you should do is only advertise products that your readers are or might be interested in.

If you are in the weight loss niche, promote weight loss products.

Promote video games and accessories if you are in the video game niche.

Promote clothing that your audience would wear, since you are in a particular clothing niche.

19. Copy and paste content from the product sales page

Quite common in newbies. Do you know why? Because they are lazy.

Too lazy to write their own stuff and too lazy to research.

Copying and pasting content from other websites to yours is a big no-no. Google, the world's largest search engine, calls this duplicate content.

Do you know what happens when Google finds duplicate content? The site is penalized. In other words - it loses its ranking (and much of its traffic). And you can't hide anything from Google online. They have eyes on every website.

What you should do….. It's very simple: always write your own content.

Write down all the information you will need when researching a product for your review post.

Let's say you are reviewing the Hydroxycut weight loss product.

Take notes instead of copying the content word for word.

20. Don't fool your visitors

What most bloggers and marketers, especially beginners, don't understand is that internet users (your readers) are 100% real people.

So if you have an ugly website design or big blocks of text in your posts, your readers won't like it. And if they don't like it, they'll leave your website and (probably) never come back.

What should you do? Start with a nice, sleek design. But don't make it too clear. This means that you don't just use black, white, and gray. Add some color to your theme / design (2-3 colors usually look best).

Your site must have a blogroll as a homepage. That way, your readers can see all of your new posts. Your sidebar should be sturdy. It should contain: links to some of your top pages (custom menu widget), 1 or 2 banner ads (max), a popular post widget, the latest reviews or posts, and your content.

Your content must be readable, engaging, and well written and formatted. It should be full of facts, details, and useful tips, tricks, or techniques.

21. Write irrelevant content

This one is very similar to number 18 on this list. Except this time it has to do with the content (blog posts and pages).

For example, let's say Bobby has a blog aimed at men who are trying to lose their male boobs (moobs). And it has about 100 visitors a month. His blog topics would be exercise, nutrition, etc., right?

Okay. One day he publishes a 2500-word blog post about the five ways to make money online. He is proud of himself for having written the best contribution he has ever written.

After a few days, he'll check his analysis to see if anyone has read his new message. He sees that the message received 10 page views (most of which are probably his). So he writes another one. This time about how to start a blog and make money. The same thing - 10 page views and most of them are him.

Now he has two messages that have nothing to do with moobs. What do you think his readers will think?

What should you do? Stick to the topics of your niche. If you had a food blog, you'd only be writing about food, right? Would it make sense to write a blog post about starting a blog?

The same goes for a niche weight loss website. And a niche site for winter coats. Or a niche / affiliate site. So stick with your niche.

Don't post anything irrelevant.

22. Not writing reviews in the right way

You're probably not sure what I'm talking about, are you?

Remember what I said in # 5 about choosing which products to review? How do I know if the product is fraudulent or okay to link to a legitimate product?

This works great for affiliate websites as no matter which review a reader is from, chances are they will go to your main review. I'll give you an example ...

Suppose you currently have 3 reviews:

1. Your "legitimate product" rating - This is your # 1 recommended product and the way you make money
2. Your rating "OK product"
3. Your rating of "Fraud Products"

Now a man named Jay is discovering the "good product". Now he needs to know if it is worth the money.

He searches for reviews and finds yours. He reads, finds out there is something better, and clicks your main review link. BAM. And then a woman named Joy learns about "scam products". Now she has to find out whether it is good or not.

She searches for reviews and easily finds yours in the top 3 of Google because you do good SEO. She reads, finds out it's a crappy deal and clicks on your main review link. BAM.

Do you see how great that can be?

What should you do? It is easy. Very easy. This is not rocket science. All you need to do is add your main review link to all other reviews.

Let me break it down for you:

1. You write a review for your featured product. This would be your most important contribution. Your main source of income.
2. Looking for products that are either completely ripped off (low quality) or not as good as the main product.
3. You write reviews for each of these products. Here you would talk about how bad or "okay" the product is.

And then you'd include the main review link at the end (and even in the middle a few times) of each review.

Conclusion

Making mistakes is like bad horror movies that people always make. Even when you start affiliate marketing. Whatever you do, you're always doing something wrong.

But with the 22 I mentioned above, I'm sure it will save you a lot of valuable time.

CONCLUSION

If you're reading the conclusion, it means you've reached the end of the book.

I hope it was a pleasant read and the information was interesting.

I hope, from all this, you learn to discover your real success in life. You will be able to find your talents and make the most of them, you will be able to combine a few small habits in life and in trading that will lead you to improve both. I'm sure that after reading this book, at the right time, you will be able to leapfrog into the pond and not into hot water!

I wish you every success in your business and other endeavours, have a great life!